LANGUAGE POLICY

LANGUAGE POLICY

DOMINANT ENGLISH,
PLURALIST CHALLENGES

Edited by

WILLIAM EGGINGTON

HELEN WREN

JOHN BENJAMINS PUBLISHING COMPANY
AMSTERDAM/PHILADELPHIA

LANGUAGE AUSTRALIA LTD
CANBERRA

TM The paper used in this publication meets the minimum requirements of American National Standard for Information Sciences — Permanence of Paper for Printed Library Materials, ANSI Z39.48-1984.

Library of Congress Cataloging-in-Publication Data

Language policy : dominant English, pluralist challenges / [edited by] William Eggington, Helen Wren.

   p.   cm.

   Includes bibliographical references.

   1. Language policy--English-speaking countries. 2. Language and languages--Political aspects. 3. English language--Political aspects. I. Eggington, William. II. Wren, Helen.

P119.32.E54L365   1997

306.44'9'09175--dc21   96-6513

ISBN 90 272 2163 4 (Eur.) / 1-55619-517-6 (US)   CIP

1 875578 62 5 (Australian) (alk. paper)

Language Australia, P.O.Box 31, Belconnen ACT 2614, Australia
John Benjamins Publishing Co. • P.O.Box 75577 • 1070 AN Amsterdam • The Netherlands
John Benjamins North America • P.O.Box 27519 • Philadelphia PA 19118-0519 • USA

CONTENTS

Acknowledgments

In addition to acknowledging the work of the contributors to this volume, we wish to express our gratitude to the following people and institutions for making it possible for *Language Policy: Dominant English, Pluralist Challenges* to be published:

Joseph Lo Bianco, Pauline Bryant and Chris Holmes at Language Australia, and Yola de Lusenet and Kees Vaes at Benjamins Publishers for their patience and enthusiasm for the project

Linda Hunter Adams and her students at Brigham Young University's Humanities Publication Center for the work they did in preparing the publication

TESOL International Inc. for giving permission for some of the papers in this volume to be published and for providing a forum for important ideas and issues surrounding the English language to be discussed and disseminated.

We wish also to acknowledge our spouses, Rob and Pam, our children and our friends for their continuing support and encouragement.

Helen Wren
Bill Eggington

FOREWORD
PALMAM QUI MERUIT FERAT

Robert B. Kaplan
University of Southern California

Introduction

In her introduction to this very ambitious volume, Helen Wren defines
at least seven purposes for the book:

1. To examine the impact of English in countries in which it is taken for
   granted (ie, Australia, Britain, Canada, New Zealand, and the USA)

2. To explore how the dominance of English impacts on the development of national language policies, the maintenance of minority languages, the ability to provide services in other languages, the efforts
   to promote first language and bilingual education programs, and the
   opportunities for adult and child second language and literacy training

3. To examine language and language-in-education policies in these
   countries and the extent to which English influences various policies
   or precludes others

4. To explore the viability of a statement on national language policies
   that could be adopted by international TESOL as a statement of principles

5. To explore how to raise issues of individual, social, and educational
   responsibilities that ESOL members must face as they are influenced
   by, and can influence, the language policy agendas established in
   these countries

6. To explore what can be learned from other English-dominant nations

7. To provide an opportunity for comparing language policy and practice and perhaps for developing a more cross-national view on rights

and responsibilities in language and language-in-education in these five English-dominant nations.

Granted there is some overlap among these several purposes, still it is a tall order to achieve with only a handful of essays—to be specific, ten essays, including one from each of the five countries, three overview articles, an introduction and a set of concluding remarks by the editors. It is not my purpose here to summarize the points made in these individual articles; Wren does so in her paper that leads off the collection. But the burden of these several purposes proves too great for the content. On the contrary, what emerges from a careful reading of the contributions to this volume is the impression that:

1. the notion of "one nation/one language" is alive and well—while all of the countries represented use English, it is clear that each has its own agenda for the learning and the teaching of English

2. the notion is also alive and well that the learning of the national language is not so much about linguistics as it is about the inculcation of cultural values or about the support of the absolutely undocumented assumption that an equation exists between "proper" language use and moral behavior

3. the notion is, additionally, alive and well that one creates and implements language policy through the education sector

4. finally, the notion is alive and well that individual teachers or teacher-organizations have some hope of influencing language policy at the national level.

1. In my ideolect, I have always taken the term *national bilingualism* to mean that everyone speaks at least two languages, though not necessarily the same two. The concept that *bilingual education* is about providing a transition for a disadvantaged segment of the population to be admitted to the corridors of power via language instruction is fallacious on two counts: first, it deprives the "advantaged" segment of the population of an important skill; and, second, it cannot accomplish the implied purpose since access to social mobility and political power is only partially a function of language proficiency. In none of the countries examined does there appear to be a fundamental belief

that monolingual speakers of English would be better off if they learned another language. On the contrary, all of the countries represented seem to hold the view that national monolingualism is desirable, moral, advantageous, and necessary for national unity.

2. In all of the countries examined, the objective of language teaching— both L1 and L2—appears to be assimilation to the cultural values and political structures of the majority cultures. As David Corson writes elsewhere in this volume: "Education often routinely represses, dominates, and disempowers language users whose practices differ from the norms that it establishes". Or to put it in a slightly different way:

> [I]ssues regarding "language handicaps" and "academic under-achievement" are social phenomena that surface in the form of linguistic deviance and are then "interpreted by the experts". The traditional assessment of concept formation is based on the assumption that, if the child does not demonstrate in an appropriate linguistic form that he/she recognizes a concept (or concepts) and its (their) interrelationships in those domains "all normal children" know, the child is handicapped. A perfectly normal child who has just arrived from a linguistically, socially, and culturally different country, by not being able to produce in oral or written text the expected linguistic forms, becomes *ipso facto* "abnormal" in the eyes of the educator (Trueba 1986:48).

3. It strikes me as absurdly inefficient to try to implement language policy exclusively through the education sector, and it seems to me that the essays in this volume prove the point. It is the case, in virtually all of the countries examined, that other sectors of government develop language policies, often at considerable variance from the policy developed by the education sector. It is, further, easily demonstrable that the incentives for language learning lie outside the education sector; when the civil service (as in Canada) requires bilingualism for employees, that is a powerful incentive. It is an incentive that parents and government bureaucrats understand. Furthermore, since only a small segment of the population is in school at any given moment, the dissemination of bilinguals may take generations until the entire population has passed through schooling. All of the language policy development models I am aware of insist that language-in-education policy is subsidiary to national language policy, that national lan-

guage policy is rooted in the highest levels of government, and that the education sector follows the lead of more powerful sectors (Kaplan 1990, 1993, 1994a, 1994b, 1994c).

4. Teachers in general, but language teachers in particular, constitute a disenfranchised segment of the population; since what they do is not seen as worthwhile, they too are not seen as worthwhile. A great problem, especially in the Teachers of English as a Second Language (TESL) endeavor, lies in the fact that practitioners spend all their time preaching to the converted (not to claim that all English as a Second Language/English as a Foreign Language (ESL/EFL)teachers are indeed "converted") and that, as Roger Peddie points out elsewhere in this volume, high-level decision-makers rarely participate in dialogue on language matters with language professionals.

Are the stated purposes viable?

The Latin title of this foreword happens to have been the personal motto of Viscount Horatio Lord Nelson, the great British naval hero. (It is also the slogan that decorates the front of the physical education building on the University of Southern California campus.) It translates, roughly, as "Let him who merits bear the palm". By using this Latin phrase, I do not mean to imply that I admire Lord Nelson particularly, or that I am an Anglophile, or that I am an academic snob who prides himself on his ability to quote esoteric Latin expressions. Rather, I chose this phrase as my title because the volume to which this chapter constitutes a foreword is to some extent about *professionalism*, and this Latin phrase may exemplify professional achievement. Whatever one may think of Lord Nelson, there is no question that he was professional—the greatest naval commander of his time. There is equally no question that he—and subsequent generations of Englishmen—saw his achievements, and those of the Royal Navy, as professional. (But remember that, at the time Nelson achieved prominence, commissions in the Royal Navy were bought and sold among those who could afford such an indulgence—it was Nelson who moved the Royal Navy toward genuine professionalism.)

It is interesting that the slogan should also decorate an academic building dedicated to physical education. Without doubt, the English-speaking societies recognize a certain kind of professionalism among athletes and reward their achievements to an absurd degree. Any ESL teacher would be glad to aspire to even a tiny fraction of the salary paid to virtually any professional athlete. I recall some years ago receiving from the Social Security administration a summary of my life-time earnings on the same day the purse that boxer Mike Tyson would be paid for a fight in Las Vegas was announced in the press. It is not a question of whether Mike Tyson is an admirable model or whether what he does enhances the world in which we live in any significant way—nor, for that matter, is it a question of the relative worth of what I do. Nevertheless, there was some significant disparity between the two sums, not in my favor. Athletes are recognized as popular heroes, more so even, perhaps, than naval heroes.

The ESL profession has not, however, contributed any significant number of national heroes or heroines to Australian, British, Canadian, New Zealand, or United States cultures; indeed, I am not aware of a single public statue, streaked with the subsequent comment of pigeons, dedicated to the memory of a great ESL/EFL teacher of either gender, nor am I aware of a single ESL/EFL teacher's having been elevated to the ranks of the Nobel Laureates. On the contrary, members of this profession tend to be modest and self-effacing, tend to underestimate the importance of their contributions, tend to be overlooked even in the structural hierarchy of the teaching profession, and tend to be perceived by their students as quite minor actors in the educational process—certainly less important than science teachers. ESL teachers have tended to settle for the love of their students rather than the professional recognition of their peers or the financial remuneration that accompanies such recognition.

Why should this be so? Is it true that the task performed by the language teacher is indeed so trivial that it deserves no recognition and only passing monetary reward? Is it the case that the world would not miss language teachers should they cease to exist? I do not believe either of these presumptions to be correct. On the contrary, at the risk of reifying the issue, I think language teachers—and ESL teachers among them—hold the highest place in the teaching profession. Were it not for the language teacher, no other discipline could function. It is the language teacher who lays the foundation for all other academic study and much that is beyond formal schooling. It is the language teacher who provides the linguistic foundation on which all educational activity is built. It is the language teacher on whose shoulders rests the entire educational edifice.

Entry into the profession

The problem, rather, lies in part in the poor self-image of the language teacher and in part in the failure to capture the structure that gave rise to this profession. In the context of the latter problem, some comparative analysis may be useful. (I shall return to the former problem shortly.) In 17th-century Britain, basically three sorts of persons practised medicine: physicians, surgeons, and charlatans (and sometimes barbers). Anyone who wished to practise medicine could do so simply by announcing his (and I do mean **his**) availability. None of these categories of medical practitioners had any control over any of the others. To some extent the field was protected by the gentlemanly tradition; that is, only gentlemen were able to go to school, to become fully literate, and to deal with other gentlemen in a highly structured social system. Only gentlemen (and their dependent ladies) could afford the services of a physician; the poor were expected to die quietly. One literate and minimally educated gentleman could, of course, train another through a sort of apprenticeship system, but there was certainly no other way to prepare for the practice of medicine. The early medical journals—for example, the *Edinburgh Medical Journal*, which happens to be the oldest continuously published professional journal in the Western world—were initially merely compilations of letters written to the gentleman editor about the strange observations and successful (and unsuccessful) practices of various gentlemen practitioners. Only very gradually over the ensuing 200 years did the practitioners of medicine gain real control over their profession. They captured education first, starting formal schools of medicine and prescribing the academic curriculum requisite to become a member to the profession. Eventually, they established the practice of licensing, and they controlled absolutely the issuing of licences, as represented by the academic degree Doctor of Medicine. More recently—indeed, in this century—they have succeeded in gaining control over various additional licensing functions. Today, the American Medical Association (AMA) wields enormous lobbying power in the USA and controls absolutely the entry of new individuals into the medical profession, state by state, specialism by specialism.

Similarly, in 17th century Britain, four sorts of persons practised law: judges, solicitors, barristers, and charlatans (also known as "pettifoggers"). None of these classifications had any influence over any other classification—indeed, if there were groups at all, they tended to be composed of colleagues who worked in close physical proximity to each other—for example, at the Inns of Court in London, which were nothing more than a development out of the medieval trade guilds. The qualifications to become a judge were rooted in land ownership, not in training. Otherwise, entry into the field was controlled through a gentlemanly apprenticeship system under which one "read" for the law while working as a junior clerk in someone's office (a place in the world for younger sons who would not inherit). In a somewhat later period, Abraham Lincoln qualified as a lawyer through a similar apprenticeship system. Gradually, over time, but significantly through the 18th and 19th centuries, law practitioners gained control over the educational system, establishing schools of law at universities. And, once such training sites existed, it was an easy step to a formal qualification system of examinations—now called "sitting the bar exams" in the USA—leading to licensure. As the AMA controls entry into medicine, the American Bar Association (ABA) controls entry into the practice of law, state by state, specialism by specialism. Similar patterns exist in all five countries surveyed in this volume.

By comparison, how does one get to be a language teacher or an ESL/EFL teacher? Why, one simply attests that one is a native speaker! At the present moment, any native English-speaking youngster with a first degree in any academic subject can get a job teaching EFL in Eastern Europe or in China; there are even commercial agencies that will place her or him. To some extent, government is involved in perpetrating this fraud on the people of other nations by sending marginally trained individuals overseas (through such structures as the US Peace Corps) and absolutely untrained individuals through various international development programs. The private sector, of course, is also active in the exportation of alleged ESL/EFL teachers.

ESL/EFL teachers as a profession have done virtually nothing to mitigate these practices. The president of Teachers of English to Speakers of Other Languages (TESOL) did, some years ago, write letters to the various Eastern European embassies and consulates in Washington, DC, deploring the practice; but he was not able to offer a serious alternative because no extant recognized documentation certifies a person as a qualified ESL/EFL teacher, and the need for warm bodies at the front of the classroom exists well in excess of the supply of qualified teachers. For example, the People's Republic of China could absorb the entire trained ESL/EFL teacher production of Australia, Britain, Canada, New Zealand, and the USA for the foreseeable future without exhausting its need (though doing so would perhaps create a critical mass of expatriates large enough to destabilize the government). It is true that tertiary school records do show course work taken, but they do not certify or license teachers—course work does not guarantee either intelligence or skill. The requirements of the several states in the USA are so disparate that their certification means virtually nothing beyond the borders of the individual state—and sometimes not much even within the state.

The members of this profession have absolutely no control over the educational requirements necessary to enter the profession (though TESOL has, over the years, published a number of different useful guidelines). The practitioners of this profession have absolutely nothing to say about licensure (though representatives of TESOL, California Association of Teachers of English to Speakers of Other Languages (CATESOL), and other regional associations have periodically testified before state licensing boards and the US Office of Education). Some academic institutions offer entirely creditable graduate programs, though in these difficult economic times, many of those programs are under serious threat, and applied linguistics and TESL programs at several universities have been terminated in the past few years. Many institutions offer less-than-wonderful academic programs. And some institutions offer no programs at all. The point is that, whatever programs are offered—good, bad, or indifferent—their content is not controlled by ESL/EFL professionals to any significant degree.

International TESOL and its various affiliates constitute the best hope for practitioners to take control of the environment. But that quest for control must be a collective activity. Not until ESL teachers as a body insist that entry into the profession must be somehow certified, not until ESL teachers collectively demand licensure for individuals to set up as professionals, not until a commonly agreed-upon set of standards exists will regulation be possible. The ESL-teaching community has not yet achieved even the apprenticeship practices common among medical doctors and lawyers in the 18th century.

TESOL has toyed with the notion of a general certificate, but so far has not gotten very far in its advocacy. In part, the problem lies with the fact that regional accrediting agencies in the USA have not universally bought into the notion that ESL programs and ESL instruction should be included along with all other academic disciplines in general accreditation procedures. To the extent that ESL programs are perceived as "remedial", or as tangential to the central academic objective, there is little hope for professional status.

The self-image of ESL/EFL teachers

At the start of this foreword, I claimed there were two problems: that the profession has not captured the means of entry and that ESL/EFL teachers have a poor self-image. I have discussed briefly the problem of capturing entry into the profession. Now let me address the matter of image. Frankly speaking, in part the problem lies in the fact that numbers of people "out there" practise—and have practised—ESL instruction over long periods of time who are nonetheless not qualified. The problem is that no one has yet figured out a way to deal with that population. All current proposals for general certification carry a "grandfather clause" simply waiving quality requirements for established teachers. Until the profession itself is able to define and enforce basic quality standards, ESL teachers are likely to continue to be perceived as an undifferentiated and unqualified mob.

The matter is complicated by the existence of a great variety of ESL schools around the world. In the USA the criteria for establishing an ESL school have more to do with providing ample sanitary facilities and adequate safety mechanisms than they have to do with quality instructors, rational syllabuses, or decent textbooks, or even a decent learning environment. In other countries, even sanitation and safety are not necessary criteria, and decent learning environments are in many cases a luxury beyond reach. Anybody can open an ESL/EFL school in virtually any major city in the world by the simple expedient of renting some space and acquiring a phone number and a post-office box. In many cases, the individual opening such a school is qualified only by virtue of the fact that she or he can produce the "front money" necessary to meet the initial operating expenses. Because such a person has the absolute right to hire and fire ESL/EFL instructors, the hiring criteria normally include, primarily, the willingness of the candidate to work for very little money and, secondarily, the likelihood the candidate will be fairly passive, restraining him- or herself from making any awkward demands regarding quality instruction.

Collectively, the profession has undoubtedly produced tens of thousands of students whose English-language proficiency has improved as the result of the intervention of language teachers and of sitting in their classrooms. Some of these ESL/EFL teachers had the privilege of educating world leaders. It is, however, not sufficient for practitioners to know how successful they have been. Not until the general membership of the profession is able to say "that person is not professional and should not be teaching in the classroom"; "that program is not professional and should not be allowed to matriculate students" will we be able to talk seriously about a profession. We must be sufficiently professional to determine what it means to be professional and to exclude individuals who, and practices that, demean our professionalism.

Some steps have been taken. There are a few publications through which professionals can speak to each other and to the larger world. There are associations under whose auspices professionals can gather. There are leaders who have striven to make ESL/EFL more professional, but they have often been merely voices crying in the wilderness. It is time to start talking about standards. However, standards do not necessarily imply standardization. No one would wish to see the field standardized, to create an environment in which all ESL/EFL teachers knew the same things and behaved in the same way. On the contrary, the genius of the field lies in the diversity of the people who participate in it. Language teaching demands individuality and imagination. Mentioning standards does not imply turning all new professionals into clones of some idealized ESL/EFL teacher. Rather, the issue of standards—not the issue of standardization—must be addressed; there must be minimum standards for entry into the field generally, and there must be standards for each of the sub-specialties that define the field. Some graduates of training programs have not been taught much, and even some teachers have penetrated the field without any training at all. Some time ago I was visited in my office by a young man with a problem: he had just graduated from a respected university with specialization in art history, and he had—upon graduation—been hired to teach EFL in Eastern Europe (actually from his point of view a convenient means for visiting museums and enhancing his knowledge of art history). He was leaving in a week. What he wanted from me was an instant inoculation—delivered, preferably, in an hour—of everything he would need to know when he entered a classroom for the first time in his host country in a matter of days. If there were standards for entry into the field, the young man in my anecdote might have been spared a lot of trouble and his potential students a lot of pain.

Conclusion

Even in these stringent economic times, the message is still *carpe diem*— "seize the day". Teachers must
- refuse to work for absurdly low wages
- refuse to teach in programs whose driving motivation is greed
- refuse to teach in programs that intentionally mislead their clients, promising more than they can possibly deliver
- refuse to use intellectually impoverished materials
- refuse to teach syllabuses based on irrelevant assumptions
- refuse to be perceived as anything less than thoroughly professional
- refuse to allow unqualified individuals to be counted among their colleagues
- refuse to let unqualified individuals take their job.

In order to take such a stance, teachers must be thoroughly profession-al. International TESOL has more than 20 000 members; parallel organi-zations in other parts of the world must number into the tens of thou-sands. It is imperative to use this impressive collective power to change the world in which teachers work. Teachers must use their impressive collective power to instigate real qualifications—real standards—for the profession. Teachers must determine to make a difference, not only in the lives of their students, but in the profession they espouse. Teachers must seek to understand the ideas that motivate what they are doing. They must strive to understand the needs of their students so that they may genuinely serve those needs. Teachers must learn to appreciate those colleagues who are professional. The fact is, ESL/EFL is not per-ceived as a profession because many of its practitioners simply are not professional. Unprofessional practitioners read little or nothing. They do not understand the ideas that underlie what they do, and they make no sustained effort to learn about, or support, the institutions in which they work or the profession to which they aspire or of which they are part. They do not grasp the place of language in the total curriculum. They do not perceive the vast demographic changes that have taken place in the world, creating polyglot cities like Los Angeles and great international linguistic needs in science, commerce, and industry.

No-one who is not a member of the ESL/EFL professional community can turn this collection of the well-meaning and the well-intentioned into a real profession. If teachers as a body do not take control of their future, no one will do it for them, and they will remain a collection of unrecognized and ill-trained individuals working at the margins of the academic professional world. No doubt, if teachers do not act as a collectivity, government will impose standards, but those standards may not be ones with which the profession may wish to live and those standards may have little or nothing to do with language teaching.

Only after professionalism has been achieved within the profession can there be any hope of influencing national language policies. I fear at this moment it is premature to explore the "viability of a statement on national language policies that could be adopted by [International] TESOL as a statement of principles". To do so would be akin to individual patients attempting to influence the licensing policies of the medical profession or individual clients attempting to influence the policies of the ABA.

Except for Australia, none of the countries represented in this volume has a national language policy. Indeed, in none of the countries, including Australia, is it clear how ESL/EFL/TESL/TESOL impacts language teaching, how the field impacts the learners, or how the field impacts the practices of education ministries, let alone the policies of governments' in the larger sense. This does not mean abandoning any effort to be effective. But in order to be effective we must first get our own house in order. Let us not blame government, or parents, or students, for our deficiencies. This volume must, in my opinion, be read against the background sketched out here.

Los Angeles, California
December 1996

References

Kaplan, R. B. 1990 Literacy and language policy. *Lenguas Modernas* 17. 81–91.
Kaplan, R. B. 1993 Conquest of paradise: language planning in New Zealand. In M. Hoey and G. Fox (eds) 1993 *Data, Description, Discourse: Festschrift for John Sinclair on his 60th Birthday*. London: Harper-Collins. 151–75.
Kaplan, R. B. 1994a Language-in-education policy: relevance for developing nations. *Lenguas Modernas* 21. 39–58.

Kaplan, R. B. 1994b Language policy and planning: an overview. In W. Grabe
    et al. (eds) *Annual Review of Applied Linguistics 14*. New York: Cambridge
    University Press. 3–19.
Kaplan, R. B. 1994c Language policy and planning in New Zealand. In W.
    Grabe et al. (eds) *Annual Review of Applied Linguistics 14*. New York:
    Cambridge University Press. 156–76.
Trueba, H. T. 1986 Bilingualism and bilingual educations. In R. B. Kaplan et al.
    (eds) *Annual Review of Applied Linguistics 6*. New York: Cambridge
    University Press. 47–64.

INTRODUCTION

Helen Wren
New South Wales Department of School Education, Australia

The collection of essays in this book grew out of a colloquium on Language and Language-in-Education policies in English-speaking countries presented at the Teachers of English to Speakers of Other Languages (TESOL) Convention held in Atlanta, Georgia, in 1993. In our roles as Chair and immediate past Chair of the Sociopolitical Concerns Standing Committee of the TESOL Executive Board, Bill Eggington and I jointly organised the three-hour academic session to examine the role of English in the language policy agendas of English-dominant nations.

TESOL's mission promotes "the effective teaching and learning of English around the world while respecting individuals' language rights", so it is therefore committed to sociopolitical action in order to relate meaningfully to the second part of that mission statement. The potential international relevance of the TESOL association's activities can be gauged by the fact that this 27th Annual Convention in Atlanta was attended by some 7000 TESOL members and delegates from more than 40 nations.

Some of the major themes of this book are summarised in the convention abstract for the colloquium:

At a time when English is expanding its role as a world language it is important to examine the impact of English in countries in which it is taken for granted. At issue is how the dominance of English impacts on the development of national language policies (and national language education policies) the maintenance of minority languages, the ability to provide services in other languages, the efforts to promote first language (L1) and bilingual education programs and the opportunities for adult and child second language (L2) and literacy training.

This colloquium, therefore, will bring together perspectives from countries for which English is the dominant language. The primary purpose will be to examine language and language-in-education policies in these countries and the extent to which English influences various policies or precludes needed policies. A second purpose of the colloquium will be to explore the viability of a statement on national language policies which could be adopted by TESOL as a statement of principles. Is it possible to define a statement of principles that would be applicable to all major English-speaking countries?

We would also expect that this colloquium would be of interest to individual TESOL members by raising awareness of the role that language policies play, or do not play, in English-speaking countries. It should also raise issues of individual social and educational responsibilities which ESOL members must face as they are influenced by, and can influence, the language policy agendas established in these countries.

The rationale for the colloquium was addressed in the introductory paper as was also the topic of language policies in a number of countries (Eggington). Country-based papers from four important English-speaking countries—Australia (Lo Bianco), Canada (Cumming), the United Kingdom (Bourne), and the United States of America (McGroarty)—followed. Overview commentary was provided by Corson, and my (Wren's) concluding role as Chair was fielding an audience discussion with the panel of speakers.

In this publication, updated versions of the original four country-based papers are to be found. Although New Zealand was unable to participate in the Atlanta colloquium, we have added a fifth paper by Roger Peddie on New Zealand's language policies. General commentaries from Corson and Eggington give an overview from a more international perspective, while I examine the role of the professional TESOL association and some of the responsibilities of ESOL teachers in influencing language and education policy on behalf of their students. I also attempt to give a brief overview of some aspects of the country-based papers in asking what we can each learn from other English-dominant nations.

It is interesting to look back and see to what extent the original purposes of the TESOL 1993 international colloquium are reflected in the chapters of this book.

The original colloquium asked whether the TESOL profession could negotiate a kind of "statement of principles that would be applicable to all major English-speaking countries". The question implies expanding TESOL's role as an international broker—recognizing that sometimes the process of negotiation in itself can forge a common purpose. Developing, over time, an agreed statement of shared principles on language and language-in-education policy could be a way of further implementing the TESOL mission. Given the known link between language, power, and social justice, the members, like the TESOL association itself, will always want to return to what should be the core business of TESOL teachers. This core task lies in working to recognise and build on students' prior learning, especially their linguistic and cultural heritage, in the learning of English and in promoting active bilingualism and greater success for the future.

The publication of this collection of papers provides an opportunity for comparing language policy and practice and perhaps for developing a more cross-national view on rights and responsibilities in language and language-in-education in these five English-dominant nations.

PART I

THE DOMINANCE OF ENGLISH AND NATIONAL LANGUAGE POLICIES: AN OVERVIEW

CHAPTER 1

MAKING A DIFFERENCE IN LANGUAGE POLICY AGENDAS

Helen Wren[1]
New South Wales Department of School Education, Australia

Overview

This chapter explores a number of key issues that relate to the influence of languages and language-in-education policies in five English-dominant nations and that particularly relate to the role of the teacher of English to speakers of other languages (TESOL). Apart from raising awareness about language policy issues, the chapter also invites individual teachers, especially those concerned with the teaching of minority students from bilingual backgrounds, to examine their own understandings and practices by:

1. **Thinking globally, acting locally**
   Teachers need to develop sociopolitical awareness at both the big and the small picture level. "Thinking globally, acting locally", to borrow a phrase from the environment movement, requires knowledge and skills with which to influence the local institution, at both the class and whole school level, to give students better chances for success in mainstream education.

2. **Helping the TESOL teachers' association work for students**
   Teachers need to be active in their professional associations in attempting to develop networks that can lead to influencing mainstream education towards more inclusive language policies and practices.

---

[1] My thanks to Hermine Scheeres and Joseph Lo Bianco for helpful comments on an earlier version of this paper.

3. **Learning from the language policies and practices of other countries**

    Teachers need to be aware that international comparisons may offer solutions to implementing more pro-active and ethnically inclusive language policies in their own situation. When making comparisons, teachers need to be sensitive to local contexts and constraints.

The chapter concludes with a look at future directions and asks "where do we go from here?"

Thinking globally, acting locally: the teacher's role

TESOL teachers need, along with their linguistic and pedagogical expertise, to develop sociopolitical awareness and advocacy skills in a network of professional support. By doing so they can influence their educational institution to build on the students' first language and culture, thus increasing students' success.

In 1993 and 1994, I was teaching graduate classes in social and political implications of TESOL teaching for teachers working in various public and private adult sectors of education. Some teachers were highly motivated to take control of their workplace situation because they were feeling frustrated. The pace of change and the extent of it made them feel they were victims of forces beyond their control. In Australia, extending second chance literacy in adult education is being seen as the solution to job losses and to the restructuring of the workforce to be more literate and self-educating for the advanced technological society of the 21st century. Other teachers expressed unease about the expectations being placed on them to turn factory line workers from diverse cultural backgrounds into self-managing entrepreneurs in a 10 week literacy course. Still others claimed they were being ignored in the policy-making process in their institution or were wasting valuable resources for inadequate returns and were not being consulted.

Teachers in classrooms in both child and adult sectors of English-dominant nations of the 90s often say they are working harder but feel less in control. Some TESOL classroom teachers, usually women, claim they have to lobby intensely to avoid being accorded the marginal status given to the immigrant, refugee, or visitor ESOL (English to speakers of other languages) students in their institution or workplace. Unless there are networks of support between like-minded colleagues, the TESOL teacher can often feel overwhelmed by a remote bureaucracy that releases or withholds funds for their ESOL programs, as each new discourse shaped by the media and public opinion gains education dominance.

It is partly through collaboration with professional colleagues that teachers may learn the resource management and lobbying skills that give them strategies to take control once again and even to move to the forefront of change in education policies that affect their work.

In Australia, TESOL association members have developed a generic statement of desirable attributes of the experienced TESOL practitioner in intensive programs, schools, and adult vocational courses. This statement, the TESOL teacher competencies document (Hogan 1994), needs to be read within a framework in which initial entry standards to the profession are clearly stated as prerequisites; that is, the statement is not meant to be applicable to induction programs for beginning ESOL teachers.

The competencies document describes the TESOL teacher units of competency under four areas. While the first two, "Ethics of Teaching" and "Professionalism and Professional Development" are common to all teachers, the TESOL-specific competencies relate to two groups—to "Knowledge" and "Practice". The "Practice" units relate to curriculum, methodology, assessment, and evaluation as well as work behaviours, while in the area of "Knowledge" the document states that TESOL teachers need to demonstrate that they have:

- knowledge of language pedagogy
- knowledge of theoretical approaches to language and language learning
- sociopolitical awareness in relation to ESOL teaching.

The sociopolitical knowledge competency states that the teacher "can demonstrate awareness of relevant political, sociocultural, economic and educational contexts of TESOL practice". This awareness will be evident, says the statement, when the teacher identifies key policies and practice documents related to access and equity that "affect the TESOL teaching context" and, for example, "provide accessible information to students on multicultural and anti-discrimination policy and practice".

Teachers should be able to identify the implications of cultural diversity so as to structure the learning environment with "respect for own and other cultures' needs, and where the student's first language is valued and utilized". Skills in identifying phases of the settlement process for immigrants and of dislocation for visitor students and "possible effects on language learning" are also delineated along with the ability to identify community services relevant to students needs.

The statement on TESOL teacher competencies seems to relate the issue of developing advocacy skills to the need for TESOL teachers to have strategies to ensure "additive" bilingual programs (an "English Plus" focus) to help their students towards optimal achievement. I have referred to the document at some length because, apart from the pedagogical and linguistic skills basic to the TESOL teaching profession, advocacy skills and additive bilingual programs imply leadership. These related issues, which could be summarised as developing "advocacy skills for bilingual competence of students" are important for experienced ESOL teachers trying to understand the relevance of language and language-in-education policy to their work in the classroom.

A key aim in my talking with class-based teachers about educational leadership in TESOL and language policy issues concentrates on looking beyond the classroom to the wider sociopolitical agenda and addressing such issues as how to:

- convince them of the need to be interested in language policy issues
- make them feel they can make a difference in their own workplace
- develop their own skills in order to influence institutional colleagues
- provide them with knowledge, skills and understandings to "act locally".

In the coming years the TESOL teacher will need greater skills in sociopolitical awareness to understand the "big picture" policy agenda.

Apart from the basic influences of international developments in the fields of applied linguistics and languages pedagogy and the obvious ones like the global economy, influences on ESOL at the international level include those outlined in Figure 1.

world Englishes	TESOL association	religious institutions
demographic shifts	cultural pluralism	"ethnic cleansing" war(s)
refugees	health epidemics (HIV)	homelessness
immigration	educational travel	"interconnectedness"
ethnic ties	technology (Internet/TV)	environmentalism
United Nations NGOs	vocational education	academic internationalism
labour market shifts	jobless youth increases	longer school retention
mass media	rich vs poor division	international English
teachers' conferences	publications nationalism	

Figure 1
International influences on ESOL

The breakdown of the old economic order, the growth of new trading blocs and national boundaries along with the rapid development of globalising technologies affect all peoples in the 1990s. The international influences on the teaching of English here listed are broad and far reaching, and exploring their relevance from the teacher's perspective and vice versa would fill another book.

A brief analysis of just one of these influences—the growth of English as a world language in the developing world—may suffice as an example. Even with 1.2 billion people speaking Chinese, teachers in today's China are rated on English fluency for their academic advancement. One of the costs of modernisation and its superior technology is to master the English language as the medium of communication. While this book addresses only English-dominant nations, there is a sense in which English through technology has a dominant influence throughout the globe and decisions about English-language policy are central to teaching and learning worldwide.

One of the fastest growth industries in English-dominant nations is the teaching of English to international fee-paying students, with all the ethical and quality issues this teaching entails. Not only do teachers have to guard against setting paternalistic limits of standard "English Only" with minority immigrants in the classroom, but they also have to ensure they teach a systematic and cumulative English-language mastery that gives access to the dominant discourse. Language for a range of audiences and purposes must be made accessible to students while building on their first language and culture. For international students, ensuring that the language of instruction and communication in academic courses is accessible and nondiscriminatory requires at least "language conscious" teaching on the part of the mainstream non-specialist teacher. One of the tasks of the TESOL specialist is to convince mainstream colleagues in the educational institution of the need for specialist language courses for some overseas students as well as inclusive language-aware teaching by mainstream teachers in content courses.

To build on their students' prior learning, teachers need pluralistic attitudes. While cultural pluralism is a social reality, too often teachers value correctness in English over and above listening deeply to students to find out what they already know. In order to explore successful pluralistic advocacy, it is useful to consider the Greer definition of pluralism.

Germaine Greer (1985) talks of her experiences in a small village in Calabria in her student days, in particular of learning from Rosetta, a young peasant girl. "The first inkling that I might have been more insular and unsophisticated than the people I had inflicted myself upon", reports Greer, came one day when she was trying to convince Rosetta against the local notion of arranged marriages. Greer continues:

> Rosetta heard me out and then she said simply, *"da noi si fa cosi"*[2]. She never tried to preach her lifestyle to me and she was never tempted to judge her life by my criteria. She had no preconceived notion of backward or primitive, no prejudices equal to my blind assumption of superiority. I stopped trying to teach her and began to learn from her instead.
>
> . . . Those three months destroyed all my certainties and taught me the reality of the pluralism I had always argued for intellectually and never really understood. If I had thought that literacy equalled intelligence or education equalled wisdom I should have been incapable of learning the lessons of that summer. My experience as a teacher in an inner city high school had shown me the folly of trusting to our systems of classifying human beings according to social status and intelligence quotient, but I still shared the common assumption that the products of good nutrition, housing and education represent some kind of progress from inferior to better. Three months living with some of the poorest peasants in Europe turned that certainty upside down and it has never righted itself (Greer 1985:xiv).

---

[2] 'We do it this way.'

Greer talks of the effect of her neighbours' non-judgmental acceptance and her gradual understanding of a more complex notion of the meaning of pluralism, beyond mere intellectualism. Teachers need to remind politicians that literacy is not a cure-all for the economic ills of the world. Even literate people may not get a job. The deeper knowledge of the intuitive faculty was the basis of the Australian Aboriginal culture long before print and books, and their belief systems still engender great respect among a wide range of spiritual leaders. As TESOL teachers who spend a lot of time concerned with empowerment, we must not overemphasise literacy at the expense of language and communication skills and at the expense of encounter with the whole person of our students. As Greer says, she soon learned while teaching in an inner Melbourne high school that there was more to many students than their literacy scores would have one believe.

Even though gender or racial equity may be enshrined in legislation, inequalities are still there, because the power and status attitudes in our society are not basically changed. Mutual respect and understanding come in a recognition of our common roots and goals so that our self-interest is their self-interest. The deep-seated conviction comes that meeting the needs of all the people is quite real to our own prosperity. But large policy agendas have to seep through to the local context.

"We need large victories so that the same issues will not return again and again to haunt us", said former TESOL international president Jean Handscombe at the Sydney ATESOL 1987 conference in talking about political advocacy and TESOL leadership (Wren 1987). What can we learn from other countries and our students that might help us in the advocacy task so as not to have to rework old ground? Thinking globally means remembering the Greer concept of pluralism. Acting locally is slow and painstaking at times.

As David Corson asks in his chapter in this volume, which is particularly concerned with social justice for bilingual children, especially for many girls from minority cultures, "what can ESOL teachers do to help their students lead equitable lives?" By convincing colleagues of the benefits of self-confident, autonomous learners among their students, the TESOL teacher leader can collaborate with mainstream teachers to develop ethnic-inclusive policy statements on student access and workplace practice in their local school or educational institutions.

Helping the TESOL teachers' association work for students

The role of the TESOL professional association, especially in English-dominant immigrant nations such as Australia, includes developing member networks to influence mainstream education towards more inclusive language policies and practices.

A wide group representing researchers, publishers, materials develop-ers, administrators, and teacher educators as well as teachers, either new to the field or experienced, are members of a professional association such as TESOL. What is perhaps unique·about TESOL groups as profes-sional teacher associations in countries like the five represented in this book, is that TESOL membership links teachers working in various sec-tors—adult and child; school, higher education, or work related; basic literacy or academic; immigrant or short-course visitor; public or pri-vately funded.

Because the ESOL curriculum focuses on the English language as the medium of communication and instruction, it is usually language-cen-tred, especially in the first stages. However, it is often taught using a range of mainstream course content. The point of teaching grammar or vocabulary is to relate them to the learner's long-term needs. While a few students want English proficiency for its own sake, many more want it for academic or professional reasons. The context for TESOL teaching is, in fact, whatever this range of students needs to know to get the knowledge and skills, the qualifications, or the job they need.

Not only is the membership of the TESOL association very diverse and its curriculum interests vast, but in English-dominant nations ESL teach-ers often link with community languages, bilingual support, or multi-cultural or ethnic organisations to further widen their networks of inter-est and operation. They do this because they need to find ways of sup-porting their students who are without the language of power the dom-inant English discourse bestows on its users. In other words, member-ship in TESOL professional associations may be as diverse as any in the education community but with the focus not only on teaching English language skills but on ensuring equity gains for students.

The obvious role of TESOL associations, as with most other professional teacher associations, includes working with training and employer
groups to develop professional standards for entry to the profession and
most particularly hosting conferences and seminars to encourage members to keep knowledge and skills up to date. In TESOL associations a
lot of emphasis is placed on supporting the teacher in workshops and
meetings as well as through publications. Many otherwise isolated
members welcome the arrival of ESL newsletters and journals full of
teaching tips or reports of the latest research. But apart from publications and professional development, teachers of ESL need networks and
a lobbying focus more than most professional teachers, if they are going
to be advocates for students who are not in a position to negotiate for
themselves.

In English-dominant countries the TESOL associations usually see language policy and advocacy as central to their work, because first and
foremost the students who are taught in ESL classrooms may often be
the most disadvantaged and marginal in the community. This is certainly the case in nations such as Australia and Canada, with an immigration policy that continually welcomes a large and diverse range of new
settlers. Not only does the association have to lobby with mainstream
providers at the state or national level but the individual teacher has to
develop the kind of leadership skills that can articulate need and enlist
support to redress want at the local and institutional level.

The motivation to influence, rather than just accept, change may result
not just from a lack of acceptance of the status quo in the TESOLer's
world. It is perhaps no accident that Australian-born writers should be
so well represented in this book. A relatively small population of mainly English speakers on a vast island continent in the middle of the
Asia-Pacific is being forced to look outwards to the rest of the world for
what is seen as its economic as well as its cultural survival. If Australia
is the second most diverse society after Israel, as Lo Bianco reports in his
chapter in this volume, then it is a good place to study language policy
and its effects in this most intercultural of nation-experiments in conflict
resolution.

The potential to influence policy directions through the TESOL professional association in networking for change may be more clearly seen,
therefore, if I take another example from our experience here in
Australia.

In January 1992 the Australian Council of TESOL Associations held its Annual Conference (ACTA) in Melbourne on the theme of "Language in the Clever Country". The theme was an ironic reference to the federal government's attempts to use education reform to restructure Australia's economy. The plenary sessions had a unity of purpose: Michael Clyne from Monash University talked of enhancing our clever reputation for a national language policy by promoting social justice and cultural enrichment to assist economic strategies. Michael Breen, then of Lancaster University, warned of the dangers of adopting the economic rationalist policies of the Thatcher era's national curriculum in the UK, policies which had increased teacher stress and reduced their morale. Mary Kalantzis called for explicit teaching of critical literacies to enhance job prospects for our client group. Joseph Lo Bianco congratulated Australia's united language lobby, which had transcended ethnic and cultural divisions to save the essentials of the National Language Policy (1987) from the monoculturalism of government writers devising a new language and literacy policy in 1990. The call by Lo Bianco to TESOL teachers to develop "educational activism on language rights" had also been the main plea of the previous day's address from Alan Matheson from the Australian Council of Trade Unions (ACTU), who had challenged TESOLers to stop talking only to the converted.

If English teachers "see themselves 'standing at the very heart of the most crucial educational, cultural and political issues of our time' then they will have to position themselves within a broader industrial and political context", said Matheson quoting James Gee. He reminded the 400 or so participants that teachers will need wider competencies beyond the classroom: "Negotiating skills, lobbying, development of coalitions, working with the media, analysis of bureaucratic decision making and community liaison". In order to ensure that language policy is not only determined by economic objectives and controlled by power brokers he concluded that "the challenge for the language teaching profession is how to position itself in the context of changing immigration patterns, wider issues of economic restructuring including labour market developments and the increasing Asian regional integration of Australia".

What are some of the broader sociopolitical influences of which Gee and Matheson speak? Apart from the basic influences on ESOL of international developments in the fields of applied linguistics and languages pedagogy are those already outlined in Figure 1.

At the national level also the policies of English-dominant countries on immigration, anti-racism, multiculturalism, and so forth have a major influence on teachers' work in TESOL. These are in addition to the policies on languages, language-in-education, and literacy that the academic and research community can influence through their international networks when and if the political settings are favourable. At the national level, using Australia as an example once again, some of these influences are shown in Figure 2.

National policies:	Key groups:	"National curriculum":
multiculturalism	trade unions	assessment/credentialling
languages and literacy ed.	ethnic communities	eg, National ESL Scales
immigration	parents' organisations	school systems [state]
anti-discrimination/racism	professional teachers	private providers
national programs	business/employer	intensive ESOL Programs
vocational/jobless courses	government bodies	ESOL services
adult immigrant English	indigenous groups	international students

Figure 2
National influences on ESOL

The Australian national TESOL association, ACTA, has an active policy group that responds to national initiatives in curriculum in general schooling and adult education as well as to specific ones like the National ESL Scales for measuring child language proficiency and the language/literacy framework in the adult sphere. In 1994, the ACTA policy group prepared submissions and responses to government policy papers on, for example, teacher education in literacy and ESL, child ESL federal government funding, teacher professional development and research initiatives.

The national agenda to reform vocational education and training (VET) includes efforts to maintain students at school or further study for as long as possible. This has led to the payment of study allowances to keep poorer students 16+ years at formal study and to a broadly instrumentalist program that links education and training to the nation's future workplace needs. The VET reform has had major effects on adult ESL provision in Australia. The current belief seems to be that literacy will solve the economic woes of the unemployed (at times 10 per cent of the population) because it will give them access to training for new jobs, if not the jobs themselves.

Studies of the needs of low literacy native English speakers at the time of International Literacy Year influenced the development of the 1991 Australian Language and Literacy Policy. With immigration dropping rapidly in 1992–93 the ESL services for adult and child new arrival immigrants also declined rapidly. The success of a tiny percentage of middle-class Asian students in high status competitive courses contributed to a backlash claim that language other than English (LOTE) background students did not need further specialist ESOL help in schools or vocational classes. Federal government policy cut the ESOL funds from the Adult Migrant English Program by limiting the length of courses and access to them. In spite of unmet demand for English courses by immigrant adults, formerly targeted funds were disbursed through publicly tendered short literacy courses directed to those without jobs.

At times of economic downturn, public outrage regarding falling standards of literacy is reflected in the print media, which seeks to blame students as deficient and blame teachers for poor teaching (Green et al. 1994). More than half of the low literacy students in the new vocational classes were English speakers with the remedial needs of underachieving students from backgrounds that did not value literacy in the past— the so-called "second chance" literacy group. However, new courses for adult literacy and unemployed groups included many LOTE background students, who might be literate in their first language but did not have sufficient English proficiency to benefit from the non-ESL literacy instruction. Many of these LOTE background students were getting a "first chance" in English therefore, but were no longer assured of access to classes by ESOL specialists.

The traditional adult literacy teacher's first concerns are to develop the learners' self-esteem and to help them set learning goals. The teacher also needs to ensure that the concerns of the community are considered and that the adult literacy and basic education (ALBE) students are given access to jobs and self-sufficiency in a generalist vocation oriented course. To the ESOL practitioners, the students' first needs relate to broader linguistic, rather than just literacy, goals as the way to develop learner independence.

The role of the professional associations in this literacy–language debate may serve to further illustrate this point. Both the national literacy association, the Australian Council of Adult Literacy (ACAL), and the national TESOL association, the Australian Council of TESOL Associations (ACTA) are concerned about the large numbers of low literacy students and those from LOTE backgrounds in their classes. ACTA and ACAL are two national member associations in the Australian Literacy Federation (ALF), which was formed in 1991 along with three English professional associations focused on mainstream school teachers. Trying to reach common understandings in this mainly majority focused English coalition is an ongoing challenge. Through the Australian Literacy Federation connection a working party looked at issues at the interface between literacy and ESOL. The core policy issue TESOLers were striving to articulate relates to serving student differences, while building on their first language and culture. TESOL specialists should continue to teach LOTE background students with little proficiency in English in language-based rather than mainstream literacy classes because it is both pedagogically and financially more effective, ACTA maintained.

Working through their professional association network, TESOL teachers need to learn skills to convince colleagues that, with a stronger command of the language of instruction to understand the content areas, they can help all their students to live more equitable lives and develop as self-confident autonomous learners.

Learning from the language policies and practices of other countries

The five nations' language-in-education policies outlined elsewhere in this volume all address the key issues related to the nature of inclusion of languages other than English in education and services to their populations. The issues could be summed up in terms of a continuum with an exclusive attention to English dominance at one end, and an inclusive attention to languages other than English as well as multiple versions of the dominant English discourse at the other. Borrowing terms from the USA movements "English Only" (the official English lobby's successful campaign now in some way influencing legislation in many states) and "English Plus" (the educationists' alternative group), one can sum up the extremes of choice of language policy of any English-dominant nation in these terms.

An "English Only" policy is evident in contexts (be they state or local) in which there is inadequate attention to social equity in the community. However, if English policy is defined in terms of "standard" English, then any groups within the community for whom English is not a first language may be doubly disadvantaged. They miss out on specialised English as a second language (ESL) instruction to give them access to the medium and to the content of instruction as well as support for education (including bilingual) and services in their own first language.

"English Plus", on the other hand, implies commitment to education in both English for social and academic learning and also in the first languages of the community. This may take the form of programs to support the teaching of languages other than English (LOTEs) through bilingual instruction of indigenous or immigrant children in schools as well as to support intercultural and anti-racism education. The level of promotion or at least acceptance of local languages (LOTEs) learning in the English-speaking background community (as measured by the proportion of students in school courses) and especially in higher education enrolments may also be an indicator of an "English Plus" policy approach in English-dominant nations.

In many ways David Corson's chapter in this volume addresses this key issue of "English Only "or "English Plus" in his analysis of language policies in these five countries.

The major theme of Corson's chapter centres on "social justice for bilingual children". In their explicit or tacit Language Policy Corson claims that all five nations aim to help English learning along with cultural/social adjustment and to teach multiculturalism, but that each country does this "from a language-deficit position" (Churchill 1986, quoted in Corson). Minorities, which Corson defines as ancestral peoples as well as established and new minorities, should be provided, at the very least, with early childhood and transition bilingual support using the community LOTE as medium of instruction in the core curriculum.

TESOL teachers must advocate for fair bilingual support for minority children—those from non-dominant cultural backgrounds and lower socio-economic status—and for the particular needs of LOTE background girls from minority cultures, whose lives are often so inequitable, Corson advises. The role of language in socially constructing gendered behaviour and socialisation through language affects children in early childhood. Differences are reinforced by schools' language policies, whether overt or tacit, and there is a need, says Corson, for language-across-the-curriculum policies.

Teachers often act as if children already have access to the dominant norms in discourse. However, minority-language groups have their own rules for speaking, listening, and turn-taking behavior. Teachers often do not adjust their own language codes and may disempower and dominate children as a matter of routine. If ESL programs address only appropriateness and "correctness" then they threaten a student's overall progress. Corson reminds us that "additive" rather than "subtractive" bilingualism produces cognitive gains and that ESL teachers must make contact with the dynamic research to become bilingual educationists not just ESOL teachers. Corson advises that one way of valuing what the child brings from home to the learning, and of enhancing the child's critical awareness, of language varieties is to reward non-standard speech.

In reviewing the accounts given in the following chapters of this volume on the language policies of the five nations, I was interested to examine the common features of local education institutions and government policies in each country, where relevant, in relation to features of the nation's population, including percentage of indigenous, LOTE background, immigrant, and refugee peoples when compared to the dominant English background population numbers and places of settlement. Other factors, as Cumming's analysis of the Canadian situation reflects, need to be considered when making cross-national comparisons. These common factors include the following:

Educational programs/institutions
- school factors, eg, local vs central control (system)
- support for indigenous languages
- attitude to teaching and learning LOTEs
- bilingual programs for immigrants and community LOTEs
- recognition of distinctive pedagogy/theoretical bases of ESL teaching
- institutional policies/practices at the local level.

Government (local or national) policies
- funding mechanisms

- multiculturalism and anti-racism
- official government-managed policies.

Reviewing each of the country-based papers in this volume in all of these areas is too extensive a task for this essay, especially as some chapters do not encompass all these issues. However, the issue of TESOL and bilingual education in the country-based chapters is the focus of my brief overview of the five nations' language policies and practices.

In the chapter on the United Kingdom in the 1990s, Jill Bourne concentrates on the national curriculum language policy. Many speakers of English in Britain's government-run schools are seen as "deficit" or "too non-standard" in their use of English, says Bourne.

Since the late 1980s the number of bilingual support and community language teachers has declined. Furthermore, recognition for the Welsh language has been grudgingly supported only after a strong fight. Of the 5 per cent or so of bilingual children in UK schools, only a small fraction get bilingual support. In fact, while some residual early childhood bilingual programs remain, "there is no place for bilingual approaches in the national curriculum", notes Bourne.

There are present moves in Britain towards a minimal statement of "the basics" with control being implemented not through the curriculum but through national testing and publishing "league tables" of schools. The British government is moving state-run schools backwards, says Bourne, "to the original goal, a basic education in which linguistic diversity is rendered invisible".

The place of specific ESOL programs in British schooling is barely mentioned in Bourne's account, perhaps because the immigration program is relatively small. It would appear that bilingual English learners have some ESL teacher support in a language through content approach but get little intensive language instruction if they have minimal English.

Roger Peddie gives an overview of New Zealand schools programs and the revival of the indigenous language and culture of the Maori people. A languages policy report was prepared by Waite in 1991 on behalf of the NZ government, but responses to it presented to the new conservative government in October 1992 are still unresolved. Part of the difficulty, says Peddie, is the lack of detail on data about ethnic and indigenous languages and cultures.

About 13 per cent of the population of New Zealand is made up of the Maori people. More schools with the indigenous language *te reo Maori*, as the medium of instruction, from preschools through primary and to a few high schools, are now run on Maori lines. However, only 10 per cent of the population in high school learn Maori. But with 20 per cent of the school population of Maori background, a central focus on the indigenous language is essential to any explicit NZ language policy, Peddie reports.

A stronger commitment to languages services such as interpreting, libraries in LOTEs, ethnic media, sign language for the deaf, and language teacher training requires government sponsorship tied to a coordinated and explicit language policy. While ESL services for the 3.9 per cent of bilingual children in schools seem uncertain and adult ESL programs are not reported, the positive trend in combining forces of ESOL and languages with Maori teaching at bi-annual conferences would seem at least part evidence of a mature "English Plus" policy stance by the professionals if not the policy-makers in New Zealand, Peddie maintains.

Alister Cumming gives a useful demographic analysis of Canada where two-thirds of its 25 million population speak English, where 6 million French speakers in Québec province learn English as a foreign language in schools, and where 500 000 "first nation" indigenous peoples with their various language needs receive support. Bilingual policies in Canada relate to the fact that both French and English have official language status. Each year thousands of immigrants and refugees including about 50 000 adults with little or no English move to Canada and settle mainly in the large cities of Toronto, Vancouver, and Montreal.

The prevalent issues in Canada regarding language and language-in-education policies, says Cumming, include access to courses, tensions between regional responsibilities (federal versus state versus local area interests), the maintenance of first languages, and of Languages other than English and French (LOTEF), and the need to develop resources, theories, research, and facilitating structures to enable better language services to be funded and delivered.

As a country with an active immigration program, Canada is most like Australia, so any discussion of international comparisons of language policy has to look at immigration along with the English-language background percentage of population as a key factor for these countries. The United States continues to attract proportionally fewer immigrants, and Britain and New Zealand are not reported as actively seeking new permanent non-English settlers to add to the 5 per cent or so of their populations speaking a LOTE at home.

In the case of Australia, Joseph Lo Bianco reports that the "secure place of English" as the dominant language in its multilingual society frees the nation to implement an explicit languages policy. After Israel, Australia has the greatest demographic pluralism in birthplace and linguistic origin of any nation, and public policy and multilingualism are now possible partly because English is so secure. In Australia there is no majority versus minority debate nor is there a large place-based group of bilingual settlers, so there is not the same domestic challenge of pluralism as in USA and Canada. Lo Bianco reports that language and language-in-education planning is now well accepted as part of public discourse in Australia.

In Australia, prior to the 1960s, language planning was implicit and monolingual, but the decline of LOTE teaching and language access rights led to a coalition of lobby groups during the 1980s to secure a national languages policy in 1987. In 1991 the federal government Green Paper, which included literacy for the Anglo population in a new language and literacy policy, had a decidedly "English Only" monolingualism as its keys goal. A united lobby managed to defeat its worst excesses. Changes to the adult ESL program however have limited access to 510 hours of English instruction for newly arrived settlers of LOTE background and directed all other LOTE background immigrants to publicly tendered vocational literacy courses for the unemployed.

For the one per cent of Australians of Aboriginal heritage, many of whom now live in urban areas, language policy is way ahead of the local realities. In the past, hostility led to the death of many of the originally estimated 270 indigenous languages, reports Lo Bianco. In a House of Representatives enquiry of 1992, Aboriginal English was recognised as a dialect of English, but in schools where the issue is not addressed and only standard English is rewarded the Aboriginal child is sure to fail.

English instruction across the eight key learning areas of the national curriculum in schools is recognised by National ESL Scales of English proficiency for the LOTE background learner—an indication of the pedagogic base of ESL in education. Large state systems of public education dominate schooling in Australia. These systems show varying levels of commitment to bilingual education, perhaps because few minorities are large enough to warrant political attention located in one place. The challenge now for ESOL educators is to promote not "subtractive" but "additive" bilingualism as an asset for both Australia and the individual, says Lo Bianco.

In the chapter on the USA, Mary McGroarty's definition of language policy "as the combination of official decisions and prevailing public practices related to language education and use" is particularly suited to a nation in which centres of governance shift between federal responsibilities for immigration and language services and local delivery of education. The dictum that "all politics is local" is probably most true in the USA, where more than 15 000 school boards manage Kindergarten to Year 12 education for their local communities and where individual freedom of speech in any language is enshrined in the Bill of Rights.

The main discussion in McGroarty's chapter relates to school bilingual education for non-native speakers of English as "perhaps the clearest indication of the conflicts in American language in education policies". Pluralistic policies may be challenged especially in areas where large groups speaking a particular language—French in the Northeast, German in the Midwest and Spanish in Florida and the Southeast—are concentrated. Recent federal funding of English immersion preschools, the reduction of bilingual instruction to less than 15 per cent of the eligible school population along with an increase in evaluations of bilingual programs for political ends, point to conflicts between majority and minority groups and structural tensions between local and federal governments.

However, many school districts provide transitional bilingual programs for two to three years with both ESL and native language support while students develop mainstream language skills. Where there are sufficiently large minority language groups, a number of school districts seek to develop and maintain bilingual skills for all students. Participation in new two-way bilingual programs using native speakers of other languages as resources can give children both linguistic and intercultural competence when "consistently implemented with well trained teachers over the whole of the elementary school program", McGroarty maintains.

Both bilingual and ESL support have a place in the education of non-English-speaking students as more than 29 of the states require certificated teaching standards or endorsement for both ESL and bilingual educators. While proponents of "English Only" legislation are really arguing about local control, funding responsibility, and the desirability of recent immigrants, they exploit the claim that English is under threat and continue to work largely outside education circles for supporters. In response, more than two million educators in the largest mainstream teacher organisations in the USA support "English Plus"—the educational value of bilingualism for academic mastery and bicultural heritage, reports McGroarty.

All nations need to move from a language-deficit model in working with children, says David Corson in his chapter. Specific constraints in a country have often been used as the excuse for doing or not doing something in a policy area such as making a multicultural or language policy explicit.

Any national government that resists the commitment to fund bilingual education programs for children on the grounds that there is no one dominant language other than English may be baulking at the cost but may justify their actions around equity—which languages should be given priority for bilingual programs? If limited bilingual programs were to be introduced, catering for all LOTE groups equally is not realistic. Perhaps, however, bilingual support is realistic when 20 per cent or more of the school enrolment is from a particular language background. If so, then in NZ it is Maori (20 per cent of school children), and in the USA it is Spanish speakers (more than 50 per cent in parts of the Southwest and in Florida). In England it may be possible to run bilingual classes (Indian subcontinent languages, especially Bengali) around East London. And in Canada, French bilingual programs may be warranted in schools. Canada is most similar to Australia in terms of its immigration policy, but unlike the other four English-dominant nations in this study, Australia seems unwilling to support bilingual services on the grounds that no particular minority from a LOTE background is dominant. However, individual schools often have some larger language groups around which bilingual programs could be fostered.

McGroarty suggests that two-way bilingual programs between pairs of students have a high success rate, are cost effective, and should be fostered. Whatever the method of bilingual support, all writers seem to be arguing that both ESOL programs and bilingual programs are needed to ensure optimal achievement for non-native speakers with little proficiency in English. ESOL teachers, Corson argues, need to be active supporters of both ESOL and bilingual programs for students. Corson wants to see changes at the local level, where he believes teachers can instigate good language policies in their schools and colleges. One of the ways they might do this is for the institution to credential students' achievement in their first language and culture. Given the political will, and the advocacy of ESOL teachers for students and community, bilingual programs could become more prevalent in schools where students' prior learning is fostered and built upon, and what better place to start than with indigenous groups?

There is something to be learned from each nation in this review of language policy. In New Zealand, policies for a Maori revival since the 1960s have made impressive gains. In Canada, commitment to bilingual practices framed in findings of local research is probably more advanced than elsewhere. In Australia, an explicit languages policy has meant government funding for a range of language programs and services. In Britain, some teachers are working towards an ESOL and bilingual services revival after a demoralising battle with the national curriculum. Finally, a commitment to professional standards in TESOL and in bilingual teaching in many states in the USA acknowledges the role of both areas in serving the needs of minority children.

Where do we go from here?

For the particular language or TESOL teacher, and indeed the professional educator generally, I have discussed the need to inform oneself of language policies and their power to influence and effect change at the local or larger level. One of the aims of this book is to provide language policies in national contexts as information to help teachers become better advocates for their students, with the aim of supporting them for first- and second-language mastery in their personal and professional lives.

Attempting to compare nations and their overt or covert language policies firstly requires a sense of both history and context—the political, social, and economic influences on a particular nation's policy decisions. With their vastly different population and land size, history, indigenous peoples, ethnic mix, and immigration and education policies, any such comparison has to be approached cautiously. Nevertheless the country context underpins eventual policy initiatives and government-funding commitments and offers a basis from which to understand language policy decisions in these five countries.

It may be possible to talk of common elements across nations, although in the area of intercultural understanding more research is required. Cultural interest may be reactivated when a group has to defend its way of life; for instance, a host society when threatened turns to its previous attachments and gives new emphasis to them—especially those based on language and cultural ties (Lo Bianco 1994). In European countries, for example, restrictive immigration has suddenly been activated as old borders between nation-states in the Eastern bloc continue to break down in the 1990s.

Prospects for economic mobility may affect the way minorities work for equality treatment. The lobbying voice of minorities, especially a coalition like the Federation of Ethnic Communities Councils of Australia which lobbied along with languages and TESOL teachers through a series of forums in the early 1980s, led to the government sponsoring the release of the National Policy on Languages in Australia (Lo Bianco 1987). The policy is one example of enabling language policies begun at the bottom so as to be eventually taken up by decision-makers at the top and therefore given funding "teeth".

While no open society would deny the importance of prior consultation with practitioners—the grassroots level "bottom up" approach to policy formulation—the processes by which the consulting might be done would also vary widely from context to context. Some would argue that language policies should be formulated from consultation at the local and small level with a view to enshrining democratic processes. Schools and learning programs recently set up by, and for, indigenous people, for example, the Maori in New Zealand, have the strengths of this approach but are highly vulnerable if they are not given more secure funding through overt government-policy support.

Good government policy, others argue, may be shaped by lobbyists, the media and the groundswell of public opinion but may also be initiated from "the top" by the researchers and the senior decision-makers. But, if democracy means simple majority rules, who will empower the minority?

Quite often it is at the top where strategic leadership may derive and may try to balance needs and resources to ensure greater equity for disadvantaged and minority groups. If advocacy beyond the local level requires access to the "big picture", who in our society has the larger view? It is possible to find senior education bureaucrats who are highly committed to redistributing resources to ensure they are targeted to those most in need. In federal systems such as those in Australia and the USA, the central government for many years has funded ESL programs—in the former for both adult and child and in the latter for both bilingual and ESL school programs.

However, federal governments have a tendency to try to use equity funds to manipulate the political agenda. In Australia, generalist literacy programs are directed to all students regardless of language background, thereby denying some immigrant students access to prior skills towards mastering the language of instruction, which is the mainstream discourse around which the literacies are taught in both child and adult sectors. By funding in the name of "literacy for all", a monolingual education approach has cut specific second language literacy programs devised by ESOL specialists. ESOL funds have been directed to the basic literacy adult and child programs which use the same methods of instruction for all their students, both English and LOTE background speakers, regardless of level of English proficiency.

An overzealous attitude of ignoring difference that we have witnessed in recent government decisions has meant that previously uncontested public policy in equity areas, such as education, women's services, or mental health programs, has not been maintained. If the government of the day is committed (for example) to anti-racism policies, it may use such commitment as a mask to take away specialist and targeted programs for individuals. In the name of avoiding so-called segregation in the early 1980s the UK government school system ceased providing separate specialist and targeted ESOL programs for immigrant young people from LOTE backgrounds.

In the end, pragmatic policy is only as good as the dollars that back needed reform initiatives. The reality of public policy formulation and follow-up is in fact more complex than the dichotomy of "top down" or "bottom up" would suggest. Long-term solutions to inequity, however, as Eggington notes in his concluding chapter to this volume, require the convinced support of ordinary people to the alternative new policy.

There do seem to be some general principles that underpin the need for overt cross-national policy, if only because the covert practice may deprive by default. Arising out of an examination of bilingual issues in the five nations discussed in this volume, I have suggested some issues relevant to child contexts in the form of an exploratory statement that moves towards a few guiding principles of language policies in English-dominant nations (Figure 3).

By the year 2000, for children of bilingual background, teachers will have influenced an education that is guided by the principles listed in Figure 3.

Using some of these ideas, the international and national TESOL associations could jointly develop a statement of principles that has cross-national relevance in English-dominant countries on language and language-in-education policies.

Perhaps the near to last word should go to McGroarty's vision elsewhere in this volume of the role of the TESOL teacher. McGroarty makes an eloquent plea for language teachers to share information and help to articulate local policy alternatives sensitive to minority values. Through their professional associations, teachers can produce statements of principle regarding respect for other languages and non-standard varieties, optimal and participatory program designs, and innovative evaluation standards. They can also act as informed advocates to influence political will and resources as one of the many groups with a legitimate stake in the provision of good language services. McGroarty's advice would be well taken in TESOL and other professional teachers' associations in all five English-dominant nations.

In this chapter, teachers have been invited to examine their understandings and practices as individuals and with fellow professionals in their role as advocates for language-minority students. While the first duty of language teachers is to ensure their own linguistic mastery and quality

1. **VALUES FIRST LANGUAGE AND CULTURE**

This will be evident when needed policies promote:
- indigenous languages and cultures
- bilingual education
  - for mother tongue maintenance
  - for self-esteem and valuing of heritage
  - for improving academic skills
  - for LOTE proficiency
  - for broader intercultural understanding
- access of native-English-speaking children to intercultural awareness.

2. **PROVIDES APPROPRIATE PROGRAMS FOR BOTH SOCIAL AND ACADEMIC ENGLISH PROFICIENCY**

This will be evident when needed policies provide:
- targeted programs of intensive ESL for students with minimal English
- targeted programs of transitional language-across-the-curriculum support with specialist ESL teachers.

3. **ENSURES HIGH TEACHER QUALITY THROUGH TESOL AND BILINGUAL PROFESSIONAL CREDENTIALS AND CERTIFICATION**

This will be evident when needed policies provide:
- minimum entry levels of specialist TESOL teaching qualifications
- ongoing professional development support for updating language pedagogy.

4. **PROVIDES THE SUPPORT NEEDED FOR BILINGUAL STUDENTS TO ACHIEVE SUCCESS IN THE CULTURALLY PLURALISTIC MAINSTREAM**

This will be evident when needed policies provide:
- teacher induction courses for all teachers in "ESL in the mainstream" pedagogy.

Figure 3
Guiding principles of language policies in English-dominant nations

teaching in the language and language-through-content classroom, teachers also have a broader responsibility to influence the learning context for their students beyond the classroom.

The ability to think globally and act locally to influence the language policy agendas in one's own context should be enhanced by examining, in the pages of this volume, language policies and practices in other English-dominant nations.

References

Green, B., Hodgens, J. and Luke, A. 1994 *Debating Literacy in Australia: A Documentary History, 1945–94*. Carlton, VIC: Australian Literacy Federation.

Greer, Germaine 1985 *The Madwoman's Underclothes: Essays and Occasional Writings 1968–1985*. London: Picador.

Hogan, Susan 1994 The TESOL teacher competencies document: prepared for discussion at the ACTA National Conference in Perth. New South Wales, Leichhardt: Association of Teachers of English to Speakers of Other Languages (ATESOL).

Lo Bianco, Joseph 1987 *National Policy on Languages*. Canberra: Australian Government Publishing Service.

Lo Bianco, Joseph 1994 Education for cultural democracy: a global perspective. In *Australian Language Matters* (2:3.1). Canberra: National Languages and Literacy Institute of Australia.

McCaffrey, John 1992 Emerging empowerment models of literacy—time to farewell TESL? Paper presented at the 3rd national conference on Community Languages and English for Speakers of Other Languages, Auckland Institute of Technology, Auckland.

Matheson, Alan 1992 Language in the 'Clever Country': Repositioning the Debate in the 1990s. In *Selected Papers from the Australian Council of TESOL Associations (ACTA)/Victorian Association of TESOL and Multicultural Education (VATME) National Conference*. Vol. 1. Melbourne: VATME. 62–77.

Tucker, G. Richard (ed.) 1993 *Policy and Practice in the Education of Culturally and Linguistically Diverse Students*. Alexandria, VA: Teachers of English to Speakers of Other Languages (TESOL).

Wren, H. 1987 Leadership and the ESL teacher: some thoughts from Jean Handscombe. In *The Changing Role of the ESL Teacher: Towards 2000*. Occasional Paper No. 15, ATESOL (NSW) Rozelle.

CHAPTER 2

THE ENGLISH LANGUAGE METAPHORS WE PLAN BY

William Eggington
Brigham Young University

Metaphor is pervasive in everyday life, not just in language but in thought and action. Our ordinary conceptual system, in terms of which we both think and act, is fundamentally metaphorical in nature (Lakoff and Johnson 1980:3).

Introduction

We have been conditioned to think of the term *metaphor* as a literary device used to evoke a special relationship or meaning or association. However, a growing number of linguists and philosophers have come to an understanding that we explain and relate much of our everyday experience in terms of metaphor. In this context, metaphor is defined as "understanding and experiencing one kind of thing in terms of another" (Lakoff and Johnson 1980:5).

In this essay, I will explore the notion that societies in which English is the historically dominant language hold an approximate common set of metaphors for the English language. These metaphors are so pervasive that they influence many sociocultural constructs including language policy procedures and outcomes. I will accomplish this task by first discussing the notion of social metaphor and then describing a set of metaphors we hold for the English language. I will conclude by examining the implications these metaphors may have on these policies.

The impact of socially shared metaphors

As a sociolinguist, I became aware of the influence of metaphor when I began to examine socially shared sets of understandings that contribute to definitions of culture and group. For example, Western English-speaking cultures share a set of metaphors for the brain. Currently, the brain is a computer. We get "input", we "interface", we are "programmed," and so on. Other "brain" metaphors include "the brain is a lightbulb" (for example, in cartoons we know that a character has a "bright" idea when a lightbulb goes on over the character's head) or "the brain is a machine" (when someone is thinking we say "the wheels are turning"). I suspect there is a tendency to describe the brain with a metaphor that is related to a central icon of the age. Notice also that these metaphors are cumulative in the sense that we still retain aspects of the machine and lightbulb metaphors in our current "brain-is-computer" age.

A host of similar metaphors are understood, or shared, by many within our culture. It is these shared metaphors that help us decode much of our experience. For example, advertisers rely on shared metaphors to help create common understandings of their advertisements. A scan of a popular magazine might uncover automobile metaphors such as "car is speed", "car is power", "car is sensual", and "car is prestige". If an individual were to visit from a culture that has not adopted these metaphors, perhaps a culture that thinks of "car" as transport and nothing else, that individual might find it difficult to decode or "negotiate" the intended meaning—she may not "get it". The "it" that she may not "get" refers to the often implicit, shared metaphors mentioned previously.

When we engage in cross-cultural communication (an activity more common than we think), shared implicit metaphors need to be made explicit in order for understandings to be achieved. Graham (1986) discovered that outback Australian Aboriginal children did not understand the "school is purposeful learning center" metaphor. For them, school is a continuation of community social interaction. Thus, when a teacher asks students to engage in an addition activity by counting and adding sets of peanuts, the teacher expects students to work within a set of non-Aboriginal school metaphors. They are to play the school game by focusing on the socially decontextualized, purposeful-learning metaphors inherent in the exercise. On the other hand, the students see the activity as a social game in which the pervading metaphor is "activity as social unifier", not "activity as purposeful learning". The students socially construct their answers by bouncing their guesses off each other. The teacher appears mystified and frustrated as to why the students, as individuals, do not just count the peanuts, add the numbers and then call out the answer. After all, the first person with the correct answer wins a prize.

Let me stress here that I am not suggesting that we are controlled, or bound, by our shared metaphors. It is true that shared, implicit metaphors can become so entrenched in our society that they become fossilized cultural attitudes which are difficult to change. However, we can break out of them when these metaphors are challenged and/or made explicit through sometimes painful processes of social change. For example, over the past 150 years, Western societies have rejected a set of racial metaphors that were once assumed as being indisputable fact. These racial metaphors made it possible for Western governments and individuals to implement policies that led to the extermination and enslavement of "savages" and the domination of non-European cultures and peoples. Currently, many gender-related metaphors are being challenged, including "woman as object", "woman as nurturer", "man as breadwinner", and "man as warrior". It may be that 150 years from now, these metaphors will be seen as repugnant as the previously mentioned racial metaphors.

As English speakers, we share a set of cumulative metaphors dealing with English that have grown out of the historical sociopolitical history of the language. For example, commencing in the 17th century, many people in England began to think that there was a connection between "correct" language use and moral fiber. Moral people speak correct English. This "correct English is morality" metaphor has been part of the set of English language metaphors since then. We will examine more of them below. First, however, notice how many metaphors of this type have an anti-metaphor corollary. Thus, if we accept the "correct English is morality" metaphor, then we must also accept the "incorrect English is immorality/lazy" metaphor.

Notice also that the acceptance of this metaphor led to social action and sometimes to social policy. Dictionaries and grammars were produced.

The children of the upper class, or the aspiring middle classes, were sent to schools to help them become educated, moral citizens of the nation. It is, by the way, no coincidence that these places of instruction were called "grammar schools". Eventually, governments created mass-education policies that encoded the "correct English is morality" metaphor into parts of government language-in-education policies, many of which continue to this day.

There are many overlapping cultural features among nations where English is the dominant language. I would like to suggest that one feature we share is a fairly similar set of metaphors about the English language, and English-speaking people, and about languages other than English and non-native English-speaking people. For example, Received Pronunciation (RP) is generally regarded as the international prestige (or pompous) variety of English; among English-speaking peoples, French is the language of romance; non-native English speakers can understand English only if English speakers engage them in loud, stilted, reduced English (foreigner talk), and foreigners with certain accents cannot be trusted, or are lazy, or unintelligent. Notice how the entertainment industry feeds on the acceptance of these linguistic stereotypes among the English-speaking world. Indeed, in a study of "standard language ideology and the perpetuation of sociolinguistic stereotypes in Disney animated films", Arnet et al. (1994) were able to show that "misconceptions about language and structure and function are widespread, and enjoy an unusual degree of consensus across social and geographic boundaries", and that certain Disney films

> teach children to link sets of certain social characteristics and contexts with language varieties in non-factual and sometimes overtly discriminatory ways. For example, animated characters with strongly positive actions and motivations are overwhelmingly speakers of unmarked varieties of English. Conversely, characters with strongly negative actions and motivations often speak varieties of English linked to specific geographic regions and marginalized social groups. Perhaps even more importantly, the characters with unmarked or "mainstream" accents have available an entire spectrum of possibilities; they may be heroes or villains, human or animal, attractive or unattractive. However, characters who speak any kind of non-mainstream language are relegated to a more limited range of roles and experiences (Arnet et al. 1994:3).

I would like to suggest here that the language metaphors presented in the media, and described above, "work", because they are already accepted by most people in the native English-speaking world. Once again, many of these socially shared metaphors seep into general language and language-in-education policies.

English language related metaphors

Figure 4 provides an overview of a set of metaphors that I believe have had an impact on the development of language policy in English-speaking nations. To some extent these metaphors are subjective interpretations, although I will attempt to justify their existence by examining their historical origins in an all too brief and simplistic manner, as well as their past and current social manifestations. I have grouped the metaphors in three broad historic categories:

- Foundation metaphors (5th–17th century)
- Expansion metaphors (17th–mid-20th century)
- Contemporary metaphors (mid-20th century–).

Foundation metaphors are those metaphors that developed during the period when English was the language spoken in the British Isles and nowhere else. It is the period that contains the birth of the language, the interweaving of the language with the culture, identity and early history of the British peoples, the invasion of England by the Normans and the development of English as a literate language.

Expansion metaphors grew out of the period when the English language developed from relative obscurity, to the language of a vast empire. This period has the language becoming a language of colonial imperialism, world business, and scientific communication. Although the sun has set upon the British Empire, its linguistic legacy continues to expand leading into the development of a set of contemporary metaphors, which, in all likelihood, will continue for generations. Consider, for example, the linguistic legacy of the Roman and Chinese empires as it is revealed in the Romance languages (French, Spanish, Portuguese, Romanian, and Italian), languages heavily influenced by the Romance languages such as English, the extent of Chinese root words in Korean and Japanese, and the reliance on Chinese characters in the ways these two languages have evolved into literate languages. The remainder of this paper will explore the metaphors in Figure 4 in more detail, focusing primarily on their language policy implications.

FOUNDATION METAPHORS (5TH–17TH CENTURY)

1 English is *our* language.
2 English is oppressed language.
3 English is ascending language.
4 English is national language.
5 English is language of beauty.
6 "Correct" English is language of moral people.
7 "Correct" English is language of intelligent people.

+ EXPANSION METAPHORS (17TH–MID-20TH CENTURY)

8 English is colonizing language.
9 English is civilizing language.
10 Standard English is morality.
11 Literacy (in English) is survival.
12 Literacy (in English) is power.
13 Literacy (in English) is state of grace.
14 English literacy is gateway to social rewards.
15 Standard English is liberating language.
16 Standard English is assimilating language.
17 Standard English is *the* language.
18 Standard written English is *the* language.
+ CONTEMPORARY METAPHORS (MID-20TH CENTURY–)

19 English is international language of wider communication.
20   Standard written English is language of information storage and retrieval.
21 Standard English is empowering language.
22 English is oppressing language.
23 English is world cultural literacy.
24 English is language of cultural imperialism.
25 English is language under threat.

Figure 4
A cumulative list of metaphors about the English language

Foundation metaphors

This set of metaphors includes the assumptions that

• English is *our* language
• English is oppressed language

- English is ascending language
- English is national language
- English is language of beauty
- "Correct" English is language of moral people
- "Correct" English is language of intelligent people.

It is more than likely that the English language grew out of a contact language, pidgin, creole process during the fifth and sixth centuries among the Anglo-Saxon, Jute, and Danish peoples (collectively known as the Angles or *Angelcynn*—kin or race of the Angles) who were invading the Southern British Isles during this period. *Englisc* was the language they spoke, and about AD 1000 the land they invaded became known as *Englaland* (Baugh and Cable 1993:49). Thus, the root metaphors for "England", the name of the land and the nation, include the name of the people and the name of the language these people speak: thus English is the people's language, and English is the land's language.

These metaphorical links were not unique to the English, except that these people lived on an island and thus did not share fuzzy linguistic borders with other languages. Note that the English-speaking colonial derivatives of England (USA, Canada, Australia, and New Zealand) shared many of these same language-people-nation root metaphors in their historical development. Indeed, when Great Britain colonialized these land masses, the colonizers not only presumed a *terra nullus* attitude (the land is empty), but also a *lingua nullus* attitude which refused to recognize the legitimate existence and need for survival of any indigenous languages (Eggington 1994b:137). English was simply the language of the empire.

These notions of land, people, and language became reinforced as a result of the Norman conquest of England in 1066. The French-speaking Normans established a governing structure in which French was the conqueror language and the language of government and law. The English language became the language of an oppressed people, and, as such, became more strongly identified as "our" language. A chronicle of this time written by Robert of Gloucester states:

> Thus came, lo! England into Normandy's hand.
> And the Normans didn't know how to speak then but their own speech
> And spoke French as they did at home, and their children did also teach;

So that high men of this land that of their own blood come
Hold all that same speech that they took from them.
For but a man know French men count him of little.
But low men hold to English and to their own speech yet.
I think there are in all the world no countries
That don't hold to their own speech but England alone.
But men well know it is well for to know both,
For the more that a man knows, the more worth he is.
(As cited in Baugh and Cable 1993:112; emphasis mine)

Note the metaphorical loadings contained in this passage: monolingual French speakers as discounted people, English as the language of "low"[3] people, English speakers as stubbornly refusing to change their language, bilingualism as something to improve one's worth.

During the reign of Henry V (1413–1422), the power of French waned while the power of English ascended to become the national language. A similar metaphorical analysis of the following 1422 language policy resolution of the London brewers association (see Figure 5) reveals the continuation and development of metaphors which remain common to the present time.

This period of political and linguistic oppression and ascension reinforced the boundary metaphors that had been developing since the beginnings of the language; namely, English is "our" language, and English is the language of "our" nation. Along with the widespread acceptance of these metaphors came the acceptance of the inverse metaphors resulting in notions such as non-English speakers are not part of "us", nor are they part of the nation.

It is probably no coincidence that shortly after the ascendancy of English, the language reached its "golden age" in terms of creative expression. The works of Shakespeare, Milton, the King James Version of the Bible, and other literary masterpieces contributed to the notion that great beauty and truth could be expressed through the English language. English became a language of beauty and truth.

---

[3] The Oxford English Dictionary definition of 'low' for this period, in this context, is people 'of humble rank, station, position, or estimation'.

THE TEXT	LANGUAGE RELATED METAPHORS
Whereas our mother tongue[1], to wit, the English tongue, hath in modern days begun to be honorably enlarged and adorned[2]; for that our most excellent lord king Henry the Fifth hath, in his letters missive and divers affairs touching his own person, more willingly chosen to declare the secrets of his will [in it]; and for the better understanding of his people[3], hath, with a diligent mind, procured the common idiom (setting aside others) to be commended by the exercise of writing[4]; and there are many of our craft of brewers who have the knowledge of writing and reading in the said English idiom, but in others, to wit, the Latin and French, before these times used, they do not in any wise understand; for which causes, with many others, it being considered how that the greater part of the Lords and trusty Commons have begun to make there matters to be noted down in our mother tongue[5], so we also in our craft, following in some manner their steps, have decreed in future to commit to memory the needful things which concern us.[6] (As cited in Baugh and Cable 1993:150)	1. English as mother tongue (and thus associated with loaded "mother" metaphors) 2. English as expanding language 3. English as language of ruler 4. English as language acquired by a diligent mind through writing 5. English as language of ruling class and law 6. English as language of record

Figure 5
Metaphorical analysis of 1422 Language Resolution

Because of, among other factors, this interest in literature, scholars became aware that the language was changing—an awareness that led to calls to "fix" or standardize the language. At approximately the same time, the introduction of the printing press into England resulted in more widespread literacy and a resultant call for spelling, vocabulary and grammatical standardisation.

Latin, being the unchanging intellectual and religious language of Europe and the church, became the model for many of the efforts to get people to speak and write in a prescribed, or correct, form of the English language. Some of the first grammarians held high positions in the

Anglican church resulting in the drive for language standards taking upon itself moralistic tones. Intelligent, moral people minded their *p*s and *q*s, used Latinate words where an Old English word would "suffice/do", and "adhered/stuck" to Latin-based syntax such as using "I/we shall" instead of the more frequently used "I/we will".

On the other hand, the "uneducated", the "intellectually lazy", and the "morally decadent" slurred their consonants, nasalized their vowels, and used prepositions at the end of sentences and double negatives. The "correct English as intelligent, moral behavior" and "incorrect English as unintelligent, immoral behavior" metaphors gained general acceptance and have continued in official and unofficial language policies in various manifestations up to the present time. Note the metaphorical allusions contained within Daniel Defoe's 1697 call for an English academy (a language planning proposal) whose objective was

> to polish and refine the *English* Tongue, and advance the so much neglected Faculty of Correct Language, to establish Purity and Propriety of Stile, and to purge it from all the Irregular Additions that Ignorance and Affectation have introduc'd. (As cited in Finegan 1980:20)

In summary, the wide and long-term acceptance of these foundation metaphors has resulted in socially shared attitudes toward language, attitudes that link English with national identity, and the standard variety of English with intelligent and moral behavior. Inverse attitudes resulting from these metaphors also link languages other than English with non-national identity and non-standard varieties of English with antisocial or non-productive behavior.

An examination of the language policies of English-speaking nations as presented in this volume and elsewhere reveals that some national or quasi-national policies attempt to enhance while other policies attempt to challenge and reverse these entrenched social attitudes. For example, Jill Bourne's description of language policy in Great Britain (elsewhere in this volume) suggests that language planners have accepted the validity of the foundation metaphors and have constructed policies accordingly. On the other hand, Joseph Lo Bianco's description of the Australian language policy context (elsewhere in this volume) reveals a legitimate attempt to loosen the link between Australian national identity and the English language, especially in the 1987 National Policy on Languages.

As Eggington (1994b) shows, this attempt has not been entirely successful. The Australian government's 1990 discussion paper leading to the 1991 Australian Language and Literacy Policy was a direct reactionary effort to re-establish the link between Australian nationality and English, as well as to define "literacy" as proficiency in standard written English. Reactionary efforts against more multicultural and multilingual policies should be expected. As the preceding discussion indicates, the metaphors that a multilingual policy needs to challenge are entrenched in society. Any policy that would challenge these metaphors needs to include a serious program of long-term public education. Failure to do so can easily result in opportunistic politicians offering themselves as "protectors of a sacred metaphor" and riding the issue to re-election. As the following section indicates, the foundations metaphors are not the only metaphors that can be used by politicians to further their own ambitions.

Expansion metaphors (17th – mid-20th century)

Commencing in the 17th century, the English language became a language of colonial conquest. As mentioned previously, the early British Empire builders came to their "empty" new lands with *lingua nullus* attitudes that contained a set of expansionist metaphors, some of which are as follows:

- English is colonizing language
- English is civilizing language
- Standard English is morality
- Literacy (in English) is survival
- Literacy (in English) is power
- Literacy (in English) is state of grace
- English literacy is gateway to social rewards
- Standard English is liberating language
- Standard English is assimilating language
- Standard English is *the* language
- Standard written English is *the* language.

Within these metaphors, English is seen as the language of "light" that can civilize primitive peoples so they are freed from darkness and so they can become more like "us". Literacy in English allows the uncivilized to survive in society and to gain access to religious texts that can lead to a state of religious grace. Competency in standard English (the dialect of academic writing) empowers an individual to have more control over his or her life by passing through the educational gateways established by our social systems.

Note how some of these metaphors are revealed by Samuel Daniel, a minor poet, who in 1599 prophetically asked:

> And who in time knows wither we may vent
> The treasures of our tongue, to what strange shores
> This gain of our best glory shall be sent,
> To enrich unknowing nations with its stores?
> What worlds in yet unformed Occident
> May come refined with accents that are ours?
> Or who can tell for what great work in hand
> The greatness of our style is now ordained?
> What powers it shall bring in, what spirits command,
> What thoughts let out, what humours keep restrained,
> What mischief it may powerfully withstand,
> And what fair ends may thereby be attained?
> (As cited in Kachru 1990:4)

As British colonial masters inaugurated colonial education policies, they decided that the "job of education was to produce people with mastery of English" (Phillipson 1992:111). For example, Britain's 1835 policy on public instruction for the Indian sub-continent codified a practice that had already been implemented for quite some time. It states:

The great object of the British Government ought to be the promotion of European literature and science among the natives of India; and that all the funds appropriated for the purpose of education would be best employed on English education alone. (As cited in Phillipson 1992:110)

Likewise, the colonial education policy of the United States carried with it the same "civilizing" and assimilation set of metaphors as elaborated by Victor Clark, an early Commissioner of Education for Puerto Rico. He suggests that "if the schools became American and the teachers and students were guided by the American spirit, then the island would be essentially American in sympathies, opinions, and attitudes toward government" (Zentella 1981:219 as cited in Kachru 1990:5).

Naturally, similar language-in-education policies were enacted in those colonies where the indigenous populations were destroyed or were "treatied" into oppressive submission. In Australia, language policies for Australia's Aboriginal peoples can be described within four distinct periods (see Baldauf and Eggington 1989):

1. The colonial period during which the success of education was measured by how many children could be removed from the cultural and linguistic influence of their parents who spoke "rubbish" languages

2. The protection-segregation period during which Aboriginal peoples were placed on reserves with severe personal restrictions. The speaking of Aboriginal languages was sometimes forbidden in favor of English

3. The assimilation-integration period during which "all Aborigines and part-Aborigines are expected eventually to attain the same manner of living as other Australians and to live as members of a single Australian community enjoying the same rights and privileges, accepting the same responsibilities, observing the same customs and influenced by the same beliefs, as other Australians" (Native Welfare Conference, 1961, as cited in Baldauf and Eggington 1989:16)

4. The self-determination period during which Aboriginal cultures and languages were recognized as important to Aboriginal survival. Unfortunately, so much damage has been done, only a few languages have any chance to survive.

What is interesting about Australia's policies toward its indigenous population is that a similar history is reflected in the policies of most of the English-dominant, post-colonial nations. I became aware of this fact at the 1990 TESOL international conference while participating in a panel discussion concerning literacy development for indigenous peoples in English-speaking nations. Presenters from the various nations were asked to relate the history of the linguistic colonization of their respective countries. It seemed that our nations' policies were "lock-stepped" together. My search for a causative variable to explain this phenomenon led me to conclude that the English speakers of each nation were functioning from a shared set of assumptions about English and indigenous languages, which in turn led me to this present analysis of the metaphorical assumptions embedded within many native English speakers. It is probably the case that policies toward non-English-speaking immigrants reflect a similar set of assumptions, based upon the same set of metaphors.

Contemporary metaphors (Mid-20th Century –)

The validity of the previously described sets of metaphors can be tested against historical developments. On the other hand, contemporary metaphors are less testable. However, I believe the following set reflects a valid description of the current socially shared assumptions that contribute to language policy development. These metaphors are:

- English is international language of wider communication
- Standard Written English is language of information storage and retrieval
- Standard English is empowering language
- English is oppressing language
- English is world cultural-literacy
- English is language of cultural imperialism
- English is language under threat.

Due to a number of factors including key historical turns and the economic power of Great Britain and the United States of America, the English language has emerged as the world's language of wider communication in most fields of cross-linguistic, international communication (Fishman et al. 1975). For example, in 1981, 86 per cent of all published material dealing with the biological sciences was in English (a gain of 11 per cent since 1965). A similar trend can be found for physics (85 per cent—a gain of 12 per cent since 1965), medicine (73 per cent—a gain of 22 per cent since 1965), and most other modern sciences (Swales 1985:2). This means that if an individual or nation wishes to gain access to, or contribute to, a huge portion of the world's current scientific knowledge, the language of access is English. English has become the key to unlocking the world's information storage and retrieval systems. Thus, the English language has a significant effect on the international scientific and technological speech community. For instance, most new scientific and technological terms are created using English-based lexical and phonological features regardless of the native language of those researchers and developers who have conducted the research or initiated the development (Radd 1989). In a linguistic sense, the world is coming to English.

Non-English-speaking nations have committed their citizens to acquire English. If a nation does not have a large pool of well-educated English speakers, access to modern technology becomes difficult. Among non-English-speaking populations in many of these nations, English has become a symbol of social and political modernization. While visiting the Summer Palace in Beijing recently, within a five-minute period I observed 28 people wearing clothing emblazoned with English slogans. I noted only eight people wearing clothing with Chinese characters displayed. Advertizing billboards scattered around Beijing proclaim various products in Chinese characters. Near the center of many of these billboards, surrounded by various eye-catching graphics, is the proclamation "new" written in English.

Sometimes, language policies in non-English-speaking nations can lead to cultural imperialism. For example, in Western Samoa students are expected to master proficiency in Standard English at the expense of proficiency in culturally important, disappearing L1 genres. On Tarawa, the main coral atoll in the Kiribati nation, students studying science must master details of steel production from textbooks written in English for Western contexts even though they are surrounded by one of the most unique, diverse and threatened biological environments on the planet. In Woorabinda, Australia, the gap between Aboriginal actual language/literacy proficiency and expected proficiency as set by an externally imposed examination system is so large that students and faculty essentially only go through the motions, resulting in high rates of student non-attendance and frequent teacher burnout and turnover (Eggington 1994a). Sadly, in spite of these failing educational practices, many teachers feel that the status quo must continue in order to meet the expectations of externally produced and externally imposed language policies that require unrealistic expectations of student English proficiency.

Many of these policies are vestiges of what Phillipson labels as "colonial language policies and practices" (1992:111) and perpetuate what Phillipson also labels as the English language teaching key tenets, namely:

- English is best taught monolingually
- The ideal teacher of English is a native speaker
- The earlier English is taught, the better the results
- The more English is taught, the better the results
- If other languages are used much, standards of English will drop (p.185).

Embedded within these tenets are assumptions that can be traced to many underlying metaphors discussed previously. Interestingly, these same tenets are followed in immigrant language-in-education policies in English-dominant nations. Given the world's acceptance of English as the language of wider communication, it is easy to explain why the world's population has little difficulty with bi- and multi-lingualism— except for the native English-speaking populations of English-dominant nations. For many, English is, after all, *the* language.

On the other hand, because of significant non-English, non-European immigration practices in English-dominant nations, many native English speakers have accepted the English-as-a-threatened-language metaphor. Sadly, the partial social acceptance of this metaphor has led to opportunistic politicians pulling at xenophobic heartstrings in order to further their careers.

Conclusion: metaphor and policy

By and large, those responsible for language policy development and implementation in English-dominant nations function within the set of English metaphors described above. They may not accept them, but they cannot ignore them. To ignore them means the development and implementation of language policies that, in the long run, will not work. For example, a language policy that promotes multilingualism in an English-dominant nation must account for long-term, cross-genera- tional resistance as a social default—resistance, in part, derived from the metaphors previously described. Failure to plan for these socially shared assumptions about English can result in society rejecting new multilingual metaphors for the set of English monolingual metaphors. The rejection process is simple. A parent complains to a politician about a child having to waste his or her time learning a second language at the expense of studying mathematics. The politician tests the waters and finds that underneath the surface lies a wealth of opinions that can be tapped to create an "issue".

Consequently, language planners need to know about the strength of metaphors shared by those who will be affected by the plan; for exam- ple, which metaphors might have the most weight or influence among the general English-speaking population, language instructors, stu- dents, and specific groups within society. Language planners also need to know about the implications of the inverse metaphors. For example, if we accept the "correct English is language of intelligent people" metaphor, what can be said about people who use non-standard English? Having ascertained social attitudes through the administration of sociolinguistic surveys, planners can begin to "sell" their plan to the general population by providing information that challenges the validity of the metaphors.

Teachers need to understand the metaphors that they may be carrying into the classroom, and they may find it advantageous to discuss social and personal metaphors with students. Finally, the reader of this volume is invited to examine the metaphors involving the language policies of English-dominant nations in the following essays.

References

Arnet, C., Dailey-O'Cain, J., Lippi-Green, R., and Simpson, R. 1994 Teaching Children How to Discriminate. Paper presented at NWAVE Conference, October 1994, Stanford University, Palo Alto, CA.

Baldauf, R. B., Jr., and Eggington, W. 1983 Language reform in Australian languages. In I. Fodor and C. Hagege (eds) *Language Reform: History and Future*. Hamburg: Helmut Buske Verlag.

Baugh, A. and Cable, T. 1993 *A History of the English Language*. 4th ed. Englewood Cliffs, NJ: Prentice-Hall.

Eggington, W. 1994a *Investigating the Transition from Upper Primary to Junior Secondary Contexts in a Rural Aboriginal Community*. Canberra: Australian Government, Department of Education, Employment and Training.

Eggington, W. 1994b Language planning and policy in Australia. In W. Grabe (ed.) *Annual Review of Applied Linguistics, 1994*. Cambridge: Cambridge University Press. 137–55.

Finegan, E. 1980 *Attitudes towards English Usage: The History of a War with Words*. New York: Teachers College Press.

Fishman J., Cooper, R., and Conrad, A. 1975 *The Spread of English*. Rowley, MS: Newbury House.

Graham, B. 1986 *Language and Mathematics in the Aboriginal Context: A Study of Classroom Interactions about Addition in the Early Years*. MA thesis, Deakin University, Australia.

Kachru, B. 1990 *The Alchemy of English: The Spread, Functions, and Models of Non-Native Englishes*. Champagne-Urbana: University of Illinois Press.

Lakoff, G. and Johnson, M. 1980 *Metaphors We Live By*. Chicago: University of Chicago Press.

Phillipson, R. 1992 *Linguistic Imperialism*. Oxford: Oxford University Press.

Radd, B. 1989 Modern trends in scientific terminology: morphology and metaphor. *American Speech* 64.2. 128–36.

Swales, J. 1985 English as the international language of research. *RELC Journal* *16.1.* 1–7.

PART II

LANGUAGE AND LANGUAGE-IN-EDUCATION POLICIES IN ENGLISH-DOMINANT NATIONS

CHAPTER 3

"THE GROWN-UPS KNOW BEST": LANGUAGE POLICY-MAKING IN BRITAIN IN THE 1990s

Jill Bourne
The Open University, Milton Keynes, UK

Language policy in education in England is now balanced on the knife edge between the most detailed and explicit language planning through legislation ever set in motion in the United Kingdom, and a return to a long tradition of inexplicit (some would say covert) control through funding mechanisms.

Language planning has been claimed by some researchers to consist of a process of systematic, government-authorised "long-term sustained and conscious effort" (Weinstein 1980). In contrast, Cooper (1989:41) has described it as "a messy affair—ad hoc, haphazard, and emotionally driven". In the past I have taken the latter view of language planning in Britain (Bourne 1991). Now the undeniable contradictions seem less important than the sustained drive and direction, and I tend to the former view, analysing a formidable manipulation of the existing contradictions in the maintenance of power.

A historical connection is often made between the perceived state of the language and the identity of the nation (see Cameron and Bourne 1989 for further discussion). An authoritarian state frequently uses the "national language" as a point of unity and social cohesion and finds linguistic diversity threatening, an element to be contained or even eliminated. In troubled times, when sectors of the community are becoming more deeply divided in terms of material wealth, language can be presented as a bond that unites.

The Newbolt Report of 1921, in the postwar turmoil of Europe, urged that "a feeling for our own native language would be a bond between classes and would beget the right kind of national pride". Furthermore, a focus on the "national language" is seen to deflect attention from more basic divisions in society. In "English for the English", written soon after the events of the 1918 Russian revolution and at a time of increased labour unrest in England, one of the Newbolt Commissioners, George Sampson (1925), warns: "Deny to working class children any common share in the immaterial, and presently they will grow into men who demand with menaces a communism of the material".

This inexplicit control through language planning at times becomes more overt, often through reference to "grammar". Grammar is, of course, not authoritarian in itself, but has come to be a signal of all sorts of other fears and desires. Thus we have John Rae, an independent school headmaster writing in the *Observer* newspaper in the early 1980s, protesting perceived changes in the British lifestyle brought about in the 1960s during a period of Labour government (Rae 1982):

> Grammar was a predictable victim of the self-indulgent sixties. It was associated with authority, tradition and elitism. Grammatical rules, like so many other rules at the time, were regarded as an intolerable infringement of personal freedom. . . As nice points of grammar were mockingly dismissed as pedantic and irrelevant, so was punctiliousness in such matters as honesty, responsibility, property, gratitude, apology and so on.

The implication is that by neglecting grammar, the country goes to the dogs; thus bringing back grammar controls the citizenry.

The first moves to create a hegemony of a national shared language in Britain are now past. As the United Kingdom fails to pull out of recession, current political pressures are more clearly focused on control, which is now much more explicit. Mrs Thatcher's original six Rs for education (O'Hear 1993) have been taken up in common party political parlance. The curriculum should be "Reading, wRiting, aRithmetic, Religious education, Right and wRong".

However, by 1993 the term "adding up" had replaced "arithmetic" (to quote John Major in a political party broadcast on 31 March) and "the national language" had joined science and maths, rather than "English" in the speech of John Patten, Secretary of State for Education (same

broadcast). Basic skills are common sense, as is national homogeneity—
no more fancy nonsense!

There is change in the air, as the detailed and gargantuan machinery of
the National Curriculum, introduced in 1988 and just beginning to be
implemented in schools, comes under attack from those pressure groups
most central to power in the UK. In its place there are orchestrated calls
for "back to basics", for "basic skills", and for minimum education
rights for children.

One writer close to government policy-makers (Letwin 1989) has even
suggested that beyond such basic rights (which, of course, should
include moral training), citizens who wish to be further educated might
need to look again to charitable institutions such as the old Workers'
Educational Association (WEA) if they or their parents were unable to
buy a richer form of education.

To understand language policy-making in this new configuration
requires a very brief history of provision for languages within the UK.
First, I would like to indicate something of the diversity of language
speakers who make up British nationals within the UK.

Linguistic profile of the United Kingdom

A multilingual society has always existed within the borders of Britain.
There are still more than 500 000 Welsh speakers identified in Wales
(Census data 1991). Mackinnon (1988) identified at least 80 000 speakers
of Scottish Gaelic. Irish Gaelic is still taught and learnt in a small number of schools in Northern Ireland. But Welsh, English, Latin, French and
Flemish were used in the activities of daily life in the Welsh borders during the Middle Ages. Society is always more heterogeneous than neat
summaries suggest. In the nineteenth century we know of the presence
within English schools of children speaking as home languages Polish,
Ukrainian, Chinese, Yiddish, French, Italian, and many other languages.

It is estimated that throughout England bilingual pupils make up more
than five per cent of the total pupil population. However, bilingual
pupils are rarely distributed evenly across local authority areas. A survey carried out in 1987 for the National Foundation for Educational
Research (Bourne 1989) found that upwards of 90 per cent of pupils in a
number of schools shared the same language other than English, espe-

cially in primary schools. Many large secondary schools have over 60 per cent of pupils sharing the same so-called "minority" languages.

In the 1980s, the European Commission put pressure on member States to encourage workforce mobility by providing for the teaching of the different languages of member States in schools. Alongside this, in the UK a strong multicultural education lobby pressured for the teaching of community languages in schools. Responding to this pressure, a number of small-scale languages surveys were carried out. For example, the Inner London Education Authority found over 170 languages spoken in its schools (ILEA Census 1989). The Linguistic Minorities Project surveyed adult languages use in three areas and child languages use in five different areas of England (LMP 1985). Local education authorities (at that point still strong, although since then dramatically weakened politically and financially by central government) began to carry out linguistic surveys of their own schools. Education became more aware of multilingualism.

Although the emphasis was often placed on diversity—on the *number* of languages used in the community—an examination of a large collection of these local authority surveys (Bourne 1989) showed that different areas had clear sociolinguistic profiles, which would make educational provision for particular languages in specific areas feasible in terms of numbers. For example, 37 languages out of the 160 listed in the London survey had only one identified speaker in the schools, and many others had very few speakers. By contrast, 22 per cent of the bilingual children identified across London were speakers of Bengali, over 12 600 pupils, often concentrated in relatively small areas. This suggests that provision for Bengali teaching or teaching through Bengali might be a feasible option in some places. Other local authorities could similarly identify languages for which provision would be feasible.

In addition to a more generally positive response to multilingualism in schools (the "valuing" and celebrating of languages other than English, a popular perhaps because an inexpensive approach) it would, then, seem also possible for more substantial educational responses to be planned for widely shared languages in different localities: languages teaching, bilingual support for learning, and even full bilingual education.

Provision for languages in the UK

The 1987 NFER survey (Bourne 1989) found a clear pattern of provision emerging across the different local authorities who then controlled state education. The greatest provision made by far was extra teachers for English as a second language support, rather than for maintaining and developing the other languages of pupils. In this, there was a swing away from special classes in English as a second language and a strong movement towards supporting bilingual pupils' learning across the curriculum and towards the development of English in relation to different subject areas through the provision of extra support staff to work alongside subject and class teachers. These extra staff were to help teachers reappraise their planning and teaching so as to be responsive to more diverse language backgrounds in all their classes, as well as to provide individual support to learners of English (Bourne and McPake 1991).

But provision for other languages used by pupils was increasingly being made. The 1987 NFER survey (Bourne 1989) showed local education authorities anxious to list any provision. More than one-third of all local authorities were then making some provision either for "bilingual support" for the curriculum or for the teaching of the languages themselves. The number of trained teachers appointed for this work remained small (417 teachers identified across 69 local education authorities in posts teaching community languages or working as bilingual support teachers, as compared with over 2500 English language support teachers identified in the same survey), but the numbers were growing.

The situation seems similar to the situation in Wales earlier this century when Welsh had no official status. Schools began responding more or less informally to their intake and to the linguistic-political demands of local communities, setting up classes to teach Welsh and sometimes to teach through the medium of Welsh. Indeed, as early as the 1960s in England, in isolated cases schools responded to new bilingual arrivals by providing not just language support, but also education through the medium of other languages where there were staff in those primary schools who shared the languages of their pupils (Townsend 1971).

In Wales, the development of teaching both Welsh and through Welsh continued unofficially in many schools until quite recently. These schools were so successful academically, including the standard of English reached, that demand increased, and extra Welsh Office funding was made increasingly available. By the mid-1980s a large number of officially designated Welsh medium primary schools and 16 designated Welsh medium secondary schools were operating.

The education system in the mid-1980s, decentralised and locally controlled, is a good example of the "benign neglect" theory of language planning, which permitted (if it did not actively foster) diversity. It was certainly far from a "golden age" of language provision, but there seemed to be some space for development, and there were some stirrings of interesting approaches.

However, the financial arrangements for any extra educational provision for bilingual pupils was unusual. Most provision for bilingual pupils (English language support and other languages) in 1987 was funded under special provisions made for local authorities to meet what were initially seen as the special needs of certain local authorities to cover extra costs incurred by working with "immigrants". This provision was called "Section 11" after the section of the 1966 *Local Government Act* that introduced the funding. This meant that, unlike all other education provision, the money for extra staff (such as ESL teachers, bilingual support teachers/assistants, and community languages teachers) came not from the Department of Education but from the Home Office, who also fund, for example, the police force. Moreover, no limit was placed on this funding. The Home Office would pay 75 per cent of costs of extra staff provided that local authorities met the remainder of the cost themselves.

With this extra and special funding available, in contrast to the continuing cutbacks made in education funding over the 1980s, it is not surprising that it was taken up by most local authorities, who consequently built up little provision of their own for bilingual pupils. However, in this way, educational provision for bilingual pupils was left vulnerable to the vagaries of Home Office policy, based on issues more related to assimilation and public order rather than on educational rationales. Some implications of this practice will become clear later in this chapter.

Changes after the 1988 Education Bill

After the 1988 *Education Act*, the Welsh Office took more responsibility for education in Wales. This had the effect of distancing Welsh education policy from English policy, constructing bilingual educational rights in Wales as not equivalent to any urged within England. Welsh was now written into the National Curriculum as a core subject within the borders of Wales. The case for Welsh as both a subject of study and the medium of education is now compartmentalised within a new Welsh Office bureaucracy and is seen as inapplicable to England—based somehow on ancient territorial rights.

Moreover, Welsh for the Welsh has seemed to strengthen the notion of English for the English. In the new order, based on some notion of geographical territory, the other languages of England become "alien", from "somewhere else". The National Curriculum now actually lists the "Modern Foreign Languages" that are permitted to be taught in schools as part of the National Curriculum. After a struggle, the original short list, which excluded many languages spoken by communities in the UK (including Welsh itself, which may not be taught as part of the National Curriculum outside the borders of Wales), was extended to include some of other languages of England: for example, Urdu, Turkish, Punjabi, and Bengali. But note, these are now categorised as "foreign" languages within the curriculum. There is no space in the structure of the National Curriculum for bilingualism or bilingual educational approaches.

Changes simultaneously began to take place in Home Office funding policy. From the late 1980s, cutbacks began to be made in Home Office funding; first to go were posts for developing multicultural education and then posts for teachers of languages other than English. Both of these were no longer considered appropriate sorts of posts for Home Office funds, the first because not specific to minority ethnic groups, the second apparently because not seen as encouraging integration or increasing achievement in national curriculum subjects. Bilingual support for curriculum learning was still funded provided the case was made that the post aimed only to support early-stage learners into the English of the curriculum, and not to develop or maintain the use of the other language.

Finally, even ESL teachers began to feel the pinch. Spending limits were set for all special funding, placing local authorities in competition with one another in making bids for extra staffing. Extra funding for posts was now given by the Home Office to bids for temporary projects, with further funding dependent on their proving they had achieved certain set performance criteria or targets over a set time limit. Most recently,

Home Office funding for even these projects has been substantially reduced, now meeting only 50 per cent of costs, with this expected to taper off over the next few years. It appears that in the current economic climate of education service cutbacks, many local authorities will not be able or willing to take on the new costs of supporting these projects and ESL staff redundancies will be made.

These changes in funding are a clear example of the way language policy can be formed by central government, while avoiding engaging in open debate on controversial topics such as minority education. Yet, if the drive appears to be towards English and the construction of homogeneity, it seems surprising at first that English-language support seems to be devalued. The answer seems to lie in shifting policies for the language education of all children. Alongside this more covert form of policy formation through funding, a huge debate on language education has recently been opening up in England. This debate has served to deflect attention from, and to marginalise yet more, the needs of linguistic minorities, since it has been framed in such a way as to focus on English. However, the twist made by the new policy moves is the insinuation of an alleged inability of most of the children with English as a *first* language in state schools to speak English properly. Apparently, English as a foreign language is for all children in state education now.

The appropriation of English

This negative attitude towards the language of the majority of the population is not new in Britain, of course. One of the Newbolt Commissioners, George Sampson, wrote in 1925 (p. 21):

> Come into a London elementary school and see what it is that the children need most. You will notice, first of all, that in a human sense, our boys and girls are almost inarticulate. They can make noises but they cannot speak.

Here the children's communication is reduced to noise; they do not communicate with Sampson, and, therefore, they are seen as not human, certainly not "civilised". The link between language and behaviour is stretched further to link language to morals. The Newbolt Report (1921) argued: "If a child is not learning good English he is learning bad English and probably bad habits of thought" (p. 10).

Again, the conflation of "grammar" and discipline pointed out at the start of this chapter is clear. Not to speak like the ruling class was clearly seen as threatening in 1921, perhaps because the rulers needed to know what was being said to feel fully in control in a situation when they were beginning to feel a loss of control. (This sounds similar to arguments heard in schools against allowing children to use their home languages in the classroom where these languages are not understood by the teacher.)

Sociolinguists have come to believe, and have had some recent success in getting others to recognise, that comprehensible English depends on the flexibility and competence of the *listener* as well as the speaker—that, with effort, one can learn to "tune in" to new accents and dialects, using the context and the many common features shared between dialects. However, it has traditionally been the powerless who have become skilled in "tuning in" to the dialects of the more powerful; and the powerful have generally overlooked and devalued this competence. Only in recent decades has there been an interest in the language of the less materially powerful and a growing awareness of the communicative power of a variety of strategies and forms of different dialects of language. An interest in variation and in the exploration of language use is a feature of the present National Curriculum for English in England. But all that is apparently about to change.

Language planning in Britain today

At this point I need to explain briefly the mechanics of language planning at present in the UK. The 1988 *Education Act* introduced by the Conservative government set out the basic contents of the National Curriculum. There were to be three core subjects—English, mathematics, and science—and a further seven foundation subjects: history, geography, music, art, religious education, a modern language (but only for children 11–16 years old) and physical education. For each subject, the Secretary of State for Education, now with sweeping new powers and taking direct responsibility for education, set up a separate Working Group. These groups worked in isolation, with different advisers and different timescales. It is no wonder the recommendations do not easily fit together within the time span of the school day and year.

The members of each Working Group were handpicked, with the Secretary of State personally vetting recommendations and even sometimes interviewing possible appointments. The leader of the English Working Group was Professor Brian Cox, the author of earlier papers in the 1970s denouncing contemporary English education and calling for stronger standards and new emphases. It was clearly hoped he would put "stiffening" into what the government had considered a disappointing report on English prepared by the earlier Kingman Committee (DES 1988).

The Kingman group had been asked to report on what both teachers and children should know about the English language. The report was received, but not endorsed, by the then Secretary of State with the damningly faint praise: "Interesting". It specifically did not recommend a return to "grammar" lessons, although it did recommend that children should learn more about the ways in which language is used. However, by then the wheels of the 1988 *Education Act* were turning, and times had moved on. The report was not what the government wanted, and, undeterred, the new Working Group on English led by Cox was asked by the Secretary of State in his Terms of Reference (DES 1989) to recommend attainment targets and detailed programmes of study covering "the grammatical structure of the English language".

Despite this clear command and its handpicked membership, the English Working Party still did not oblige. Cox, naively perhaps, was disillusioned by the experience and has written about the machinations and pressures surrounding the Working Group (Cox 1992). He has not been asked to take part in further deliberations.

The collected opinions, then, of two committees, both containing business people, writers, and teachers as well as linguists, were dismissed as the pressure for the return of grammar teaching continued unabated. Yet another new committee was set up in 1992 by the National Curriculum Council at a new Secretary of State's request. A spate of resignations followed, with members complaining that discussions were curtailed, meetings infrequent, and reading matter confined to right-wing policy centre pamphlets. The committee was still sitting when documents were leaked first to the press, then more widely, from an unknown source, purporting to be proposals for new Orders for English, already written.

Whilst the Kingman and Cox reports defined standard English as one dialect among many which, historically, had become valued because of its use across a number of prestigious domains, the proposed Orders, when they emerged (DFE 1993), defined standard English as "grammatically correct language spoken in any accent". We may have the Welsh to thank for retaining the last bit of that definition. Nevertheless, although "accent" seems to have reluctantly been accepted, "clear pronunciation" is required from the first primary years. The concept of "spoken standard English" is treated as if entirely unproblematic.

"Grammar" itself was defined as "the correct use of the standard language". (You will note the circularity in the definitions of grammar and standard English.) The proposals accepted the advice that spoken language differs from written language in having features such as hesitation and false starts, but they pointed out that the aim of the curriculum should be to "improve the fluency and accuracy" of spoken English. Children were to learn to speak written language, it seems. The weight of prescription, indeed, seems to fall on spoken rather than written language, where the emphasis seems to be placed more on correct spelling and punctuation. "Grammar" is included in the "communication" strand of the curriculum.

The previous National Curriculum English Working Group Report (DES 1989) had described the dialectal differences in English which marked some (that is, working class) social group membership as being simply "a social irritant" to some people (paragraph 4.14): forms such as "we was; he ain't done it; she come here yesterday; they never saw nobody", etc. While the Working Group insisted that every child had a right to be taught standard English, it also pointed out (in bold print) that "all these forms are grammatical and rule-governed in non-standard dialects, but the rules are different from those of Standard English" (paragraph 4.14).

This paragraph was clearly an "irritant" to right-wing policy groups. The 1993 Draft Orders (DFE 1993) laid out in detail just what children should not be allowed to say, and it entirely contradicted the linguists advising the English Working Group.

Here are some examples: At Level two Key Stage one (average age 6 to 7 years) the Programmes of Study for Speaking and Listening state "the key features of English grammar in this key stage are subject–verb agreement, effective word order and correct and consistent use of verb tenses" (DFE 1993:10). Examples given of what is required as spoken standard English in Key Stage one are "subject–verb agreement: 'We were (not was) late back from the trip'; irregular verbs: 'we won (not winned) at cricket' " (DFE 1993:13). (Remember, this is not a teachers' guide we are considering here, but proposals for statutory Orders—the law of the land.)

At Key Stage two Level four (average age 9 to 10 years) the Programme of Study for Speaking and Listening includes "acceptable standard forms of the negative; correct use of plurals; correct use of pronouns" (p. 14). Examples of incorrect usage given are " 'three miles' not 'three mile'; . . .'pass me those (not them) books!', 'Clive and I (not me) are going to Wembley'; . . . 'We haven't seen anybody (not nobody)' " (p. 17).

Only at Key Stages three and four (average age 11–16 years) is some ambiguity allowed to creep into English education. At this stage, pupils may be taught to "appreciate the use of non-standard forms for effect (eg, 'You ain't seen nothing yet!'—interestingly, I would see this as an Americanism rather than an example of permitted English dialect, and perhaps that is why it is permissible) and should recognise attitudes to language usage (such as split infinitives and different *from* rather than different *to*) which have achieved a degree of acceptability but in some circumstances attract criticism" (p. 18). Also only at Key Stages three and four is variation in language use introduced: that "the meanings and usage of words change over time", that words from other languages "are borrowed" by English, and that "vocabulary and grammar vary between standard English and dialect" (p. 18).

This completely reverses the sort of language awareness curriculum offered in the English Working Group Report (DES 1989), where young children first carry out investigations into language use in their environment, and then, with increased language awareness, come to focus directly on the features of standard English and dialectal differences from it, thus learning to extend their own continuum of language use without denying the validity of their own and their families' language (Carter 1991; National Oracy Project 1991). Many English teachers, initially suspicious of the English Working Group Report, have become enthusiastic about the sorts of results language awareness work (and, particularly, critical approaches to language awareness work) have been achieving, not only in the secondary schools, but also with very young pupils. These approaches have often taken account of the resources bilingual children bring to knowledge about language, legitimating and extending their knowledge, and recognising their achievements.

Unfortunately, the 1993 Proposals did not extend such work but seemed to aim only at eradicating various odd dialectal expressions apparently considered to be socially unacceptable.

Implications for bilingual and bi-dialectal pupils

The existence of bilingual pupils was not acknowledged in the 1993 Proposals (DFE 1993). It is important to remember that, as discussed earlier in this paper, learners of English are now integrated into the subject classroom alongside their peers. Any failure by them to jump the hurdles of the grammatical prescriptions in a system in which progress is assessed by national testing based on such Orders seems likely to mean that pupils are kept back at the lower levels of the curriculum. The implications of trying to teach the national curriculum are already seen as demanding a return to "streaming" children—that is, testing and grouping them in separate classes according to their tested achievements. The Secretary of State has already written a circular to all primary schools (February 1993) urging them to reconsider instituting streaming or setting.

Research in the 1950s and 1960s, when streaming was prevalent in the UK, confirmed that grouping children by "ability" in fact acted as a covert form of social selection, children with fathers in unskilled jobs having a far greater statistical chance of being found in the lower streams (Jackson 1964; Barker-Lunn 1970). Once children were streamed, researchers found lower expectations for children in B or C streams, with the achievement gap between the A groups and C groups rapidly widening as a result of different teaching approaches, with consequently little movement between streams once allocated.

Where language issues have become invisible, it is all too easy to recategorise learners of English as "slow learners". In an ethnographic case study of a multilingual classroom I have collected detailed evidence of how this is done (Bourne 1992). In this context, it seems clear that should the 1993 English Orders, or others like them, come into effect as the basis for assessing pupils' Levels of Attainment, pupils newly arrived in England or still at an early stage of learning English would wind up in the lower "ability" streams. Alternatively, the nature of ESL support provision could be changed to respond to a streamed situation, with separate ESL streams for pupils at an early stage of learning English. Then, once again, as was observed in the 1960s and 1970s, bilingual children might begin a career in a separate ESL language stream from which they are unlikely to emerge, since however well their English improves, they will have great difficulty in catching up on the various test hurdles being leapt over by their peers across all the curriculum subjects while they are toiling away at meeting the norms set for them in English grammar.

Back to the basics

There is a concerted effort from the various right-wing policy groups in the 1990s to abandon the National Curriculum entirely. It is seen as too expensive, overprescriptive, and opposed to the market ethic of parental choice and diversity of provision. The alternative is proposed to be "short and simple unseen national tests, based on the limited content of a revised national curriculum" (O'Hear 1993:23). Control would not be through the curriculum, but (less explicitly and therefore more efficiently) through the importance of competitive test results for pupils in a recession with a limited job market and cutbacks on higher education places, and for teachers, with schools ranked in League Tables according to results. The thinness of the resulting curriculum in an underfunded state education sector would be distanced from the government by "being left to teachers to decide". In Letwin's terms (quoted earlier), grounding would be all.

The battle over the English curriculum is still continuing in this context. A consultation process carried out by the National Curriculum Council following the publication of the proposals for revised Orders for English found that 49 per cent of those consulted (from schools, teachers' and advisers' associations, parents and governors, higher education and others) disagreed with the proposals on standard English. Of these, 25 per cent added the comment that standard English should be required when appropriate, rather than irrespective of context (NCC 1993a). However, even within the "slimmed down" National Curriculum now being implemented (DFE 1995), the emphasis on "correctness" in English usage is being emphasised even more strongly as a fundamental basic skill.

However, the struggle to define and determine an appropriate language education also takes place in the classroom itself. In the bleak picture painted here of the UK there would be some bright spots if we could include descriptions of innovative classroom practice, which, of course, continues. However, that is not the purpose of this chapter, where the focus is on national policy formation. To give some idea of the extent of opposition to such innovations, however, I need to explain that a large-scale Department of Education funded national project on "Language in the National Curriculum" (LINC), which chose to develop investigations into language based on children's own experience of language use rather than to focus on teaching formal grammar to teachers, was refused permission to publish the in-service materials produced, as they were not approved of by the then Secretary of State. (Some details of the project can be found in Carter 1991.) The stranglehold on the teaching profession is strong.

Nevertheless, professional advice from teachers can still influence national policy formation. The National Curriculum Council reconsidered the way in which progression in standard English had been tied to Levels of Attainment in the earlier proposals (DFE 1993) as a result of the consultation exercise with teachers and the public. They argued that progression in standard English could not convincingly be described within the 10 level scale, thus giving teachers rather more flexibility in their approach to spoken English.

Yet more definitions of standard English and sets of Levels of Attainment have been proposed by the NCC following these consultations (NCC 1993b). The concern revealed in the consultation exercise over requirements for standard English for pupils at Key Stage one (5–7 years) was not responded to, the new proposals stating firmly that "pupils are required to use standard English from Key Stage one" (NCC 1993b, paragraph 3.6). However, even before these could be approved, yet another new curriculum advisory body led by Sir Ron Dearing had been set up by the government, this time with the aim of "slimming down" the statutory curriculum by defining the "basics", the essential core—clearly hoping to move back to the political far-right groups' original aim for the National Curriculum (see Letwin 1989 and earlier discussion in this paper).

Thus, working group after working group has discussed, consulted, and advised—a process of attrition that has left teachers and teacher groups exhausted and apathetic. But at last we seem to be nearing the original goal. This seems to consist of designing a basic education in which linguistic diversity is rendered invisible—a basic education that can be defined as "good enough for some" in the state-controlled schools, while those more fortunate opt out (saving the state yet more money) to buy themselves richer forms of education.

The novelist Ian McEwan in *The Child in Time*, a prescient novel published in 1987, describes the way in a Britain "sometime in the future", "quangos" of the great and the good are set up on educational issues to prepare the nation for change. Meanwhile, anonymous civil servants work feverishly on alternative documents, which are leaked at appropriate moments to deflect attention from unsatisfactory reports, heightening tension and manipulating the debate onto new levels that would have been considered impossible before. Whatever the committees, the experts, the professionals, the public may think, the "grown-ups know best".

The reality is, however, that the United Kingdom is multilingual, and is likely to become more rather than less so. Researchers and writers, whatever the terms of their contracts and the parameters of their project frameworks, need to keep saying so—pointing out the political aims that underlie educational policies—if we are to crack the ideology of homogeneity that is so powerfully being constructed. Teachers in the classroom need all the support possible to make sense of the contradictions between the rhetoric and the evidence of their experience on how learning takes place and the role of language in that learning. For, finally, it is they who will implement educational policy, and it is through the manifest contradictions of the present proposals and in the public debate which has ensued that awareness of language can be increased and space created for innovative and positive approaches.

References

Barker-Lunn, J. 1970 *Streaming in the Primary School*. Slough: NFER.

Bourne, J. 1989 *Moving into the Mainstream: Provision for Bilingual Pupils*. Windsor: NFER Nelson.

Bourne, J. 1991 Languages in the school systems of England and Wales. *Linguistics and Education* 3. 81–102.

Bourne, J. 1992 *Inside a Multilingual Primary Classroom: A Teacher, Pupils and Theories at Work*. PhD thesis, University of Southampton.

Bourne, J. and McPake 1991 *Partnership Teaching: Co-operative Teaching Strategies for English Language Support in Multilingual Classes*. London: HMSO.

Cameron, D. and Bourne, J. 1989 No common ground: Kingman, Grammar and Nation. *Language and Education* 2.3. 147–60.

Carter, R. (ed.) 1991 *Knowledge about Language and the Curriculum*. London: Hodder and Stoughton.

Cooper, R. 1989 *Language Planning and Social Change*. Cambridge: Cambridge University Press.

Cox, B. 1991 *Cox on Cox: An English Curriculum for the 1990s*. London: Hodder and Stoughton.

Crowley, T. 1989 *The Politics of Discourse*. London: Macmillan.

DES 1988 *Report of the Committee of Inquiry into the Teaching of the English Language (The Kingman Report)*. London: HMSO.

DES/Welsh Office 1989 *English for Ages 5–16 (The Cox Report)*. London: HMSO.

DES/Welsh Office 1990 *Modern Foreign Languages for Ages 11–16*. London: DES/Welsh Office.

DFE/Welsh Office 1993 *English for Ages 5–16 (1993)*. London: DFE/WO.

DFE 1995 *English in the National Curriculum*. London: HMSO.

Jackson, B. 1964 *Streaming: An Education System in Miniature*. London: Routledge and Kegan Paul.

Letwin, O. 1989 Grounding comes first. In B. Moon, P. Murphy and J. Raynor (eds) *Policies for the Curriculum*. London: Open University Press.

Linguistic Minorities Project 1985 The Other Languages of England. London: Routledge and Kegan Paul.

McEwan, I. 1987 *The Child in Time*. London: Jonathan Cape.

Mackinnon, K. 1988 *An End of Ane Auld Sang—or New Dawn?* Paper presented at the British Sociological Association conference in Edinburgh, mimeo.

National Curriculum Council 1993a *Recommendations for a Revised Curriculum for English*. York: NCC.

National Curriculum Council 1993b *English: National Curriculum Council Consultation Report*. York: NCC.

Newbolt, H. 1921 *The Teaching of English in England (The Newbolt Report)*. London: HMSO.

O'Hear, A. 1993 *An Entitlement to Knowledge*. London: Centre for Policy Studies.

Rae, J. 1982 *The decline and fall of English grammar*. In The Observer 7.2.

Sampson, G. 1925 *English for the English*. London: English Association.

Townsend, H. 1971 *Immigrant Pupils in England*. Windsor: NFER Nelson.

Weinstein, B. 1980 Language planning in Franco-phone Africa. *Language Problems and Language Planning* 4. 55–77.

CHAPTER 4

LANGUAGE POLICY IN THE USA: NATIONAL VALUES, LOCAL LOYALTIES, PRAGMATIC PRESSURES

Mary McGroarty[4]
Northern Arizona University

A definition and framework: no official, but multiple, informal policies

Language policy can be defined as the combination of official decisions and prevailing public practices related to language education and use. It includes both language planning, defined as "deliberate efforts to influence the behavior of others with respect to the acquisition, structure, or functional allocation of language codes" (Cooper 1989:45), and language practices related to language learning and use which, though unofficial and occasionally inadvertent, are widespread. To characterize language policy in the USA, particularly with respect to language-related services in education, is to try to bring some coherence to a mosaic of interlocking and overlapping pieces. Reasons for the diffuse approach are many, though two stand out. First are the tensions inherent in the public ideologies related to language, which are strongly individualistic and pragmatic in character, though they include some provisions for protection of minority rights and implicit connections to the notion of pluralism. Second is the effect of the overlapping governance structures that affect all levels of education.

In this essay I will show how the provision of language services in education is affected by the co-existence of differing ideologies about language and the relatively loose coupling between levels of governance.

---

[4] My thanks to Doug Biber, Bill Grabe, and Mary Ann Steger, colleagues whose comments have helped to refine and extend the discussion here.

The uneasy equilibrium evinced in public decisions related to language in the USA is a direct result of differing ideologies about language implemented through government structures that depend on majority support but allow for, and sometimes require, certain minority rights and protections.

Many, though not all, of the tensions surrounding matters of language education and use arise from conflicts between ideologies and practices reflecting some degree of pluralism for certain groups, on the one hand, and structures of government and governance in educational institutions that function via the rule of a simple majority (as do most institutions shaping American social and political life), on the other. The ways these conflicts play out in different arenas of education illustrate the multiple factors shaping the few formal and many informal language policies now in force in the USA. In this discussion, I concentrate mainly on the interplay of different groups involved in bilingual education for non-native speakers, elementary and secondary, for it is this issue that has generated most of the recent public debate in the USA. I then briefly address other language and language-in-education policies, mainly those related to foreign language instruction for English speakers and provision of language training for adults, insofar as they further illustrate pertinent themes of the tensions between national values, community loyalties, multiple levels of educational governance, and individual rights.

Educational governance: national or local?

The USA's constitutional framework creates a general co-existence and some conflict between the multiple levels of governance, giving the federal government a central role in certain national and interstate arenas but reserving many crucial areas of governance to the states. The federal government's explicit role is to regulate international domains such as international trade and immigration, each of which has implications, actual and potential, for language-in-education policy. At the same time, governance of education, the principal arena for formal language services, is fragmented by over 150 years of practice granting main authority to local school boards and educational agencies, now numbering 15 653 at the Kindergarten to twelfth grade level alone (NCES 1992). Following Tip O'Neill's dictum that "all politics is local", one could try to explain American language-in-education policies as the sum of purely local decisions.

Yet this decentralization is only part of the picture. Actual delivery of education and other services—in areas as mundane as job training, unemployment assistance, and the issuing of drivers' licenses as well as the larger systems of health care, welfare, and criminal justice—is mediated by a system of local and regional values and practices that have, to various degrees, sometimes taken language diversity into account, both historically and currently (Cloonan and Strine 1991). The degree of latitude permitted various local institutions, both governmental and private, has allowed for some diversification of language services on a relatively "unplanned" basis (Baldauf 1994). Furthermore, national values play a role in all language-related policies. Americans' views of language use are fundamentally pragmatic (Heath 1988); if use of a language other than English is the most efficient or natural way for an individual to accomplish a task, this is tolerated if not encouraged; if freedom of self-expression includes use of a language in addition to English, it is protected. The balances and tensions that exist between various levels of institutional authority are all framed by the larger scheme of widely held though often inchoate American beliefs with respect to the various individual freedoms expressed in the Bill of Rights.

Whether commentators take a liberal or conservative position on language issues, each side seems to accept the assumption that language is not in itself a separate right; rather, insofar as it is one aspect of individual freedom of behavior protected under the Constitution, it is what might be termed a "derivative" right (Sonntag and Pool 1987). Hence, if individual self-expression includes use of another language instead of, or along side of, English, it is the right of self-expression that will be emphasized and, in litigation, protected by law (Leibowitz 1982). Where the rights of others to a presumed greater good such as health, safety, or efficient communication in a business or government setting are thought to be adversely affected by use of languages other than English, such rights can then be used to regulate language in those settings. Thus, an individual's choice of language is not an absolute right but one subject to situational constraints (Piatt 1990, 1993).

Regional and ethnic influences, historical and contemporary

Mediating between national values, federal responsibilities, local educational institutions, and individual rights are the historical forces that have foregrounded language issues at various times in different locations throughout United States history. These include patterns of early settlement, migration, and annexation of territory bringing speakers of English and other languages into contact (sometimes violent) with each other. Such cultural and linguistic contacts have had differential historical impact in regions of the country where groups of speakers of other languages were once or are still numerous: French in the Northeast, German in the Midwest, Spanish in Florida and the Southwest are common historical examples, along with the hundreds of indigenous languages once found throughout the country. Generally, where such groups enjoyed a measure of political power in local institutions, their languages were employed in local institutions. In the case of German, public schools added German to their curricula with the specific intent of attracting German students away from parochial schools (Schlossman 1983). Indigenous languages enjoyed no such status historically; used in some missionary efforts, they had no role in government-provided education until the 1930s, and even then it was short lived. The educational status of the English creoles, ranging from Gullah to Hawaiian Creole English to African-American English, has followed a course somewhat parallel to that of indigenous languages. Ridiculed for centuries, they are now gaining acceptance and recognition within the professional linguistic community as independent systems of communication with their own conventions. Academic acceptance, though, does not imply educational approbation. School systems serving large numbers of students who use these varieties expend may considerable energy in promoting bi-dialectalism with standard English. At present, Spanish in the Southwest and major urban areas claims most attention, though the vitality of Asian languages in cities of recent settlement or secondary migration, of some immigrant languages such as Haitian Creole and Russian in certain urban areas, and of some indigenous languages in native communities, contributes to contemporary linguistic diversity.

Such diverse historical contacts have created long-standing regional loyalties underlying the tolerance and promotion of, attitudes toward, and actual use of certain languages and language varieties. These loyalties in turn create networks of latent support for different approaches to language services and language education tapped at times by public decisions about language in education. Until recently the current national stance on language, as realized through the voting patterns of the United States Congress, revealed no overriding consensus on language issues, but many regional and ethnic interest clusters. A recent examination of language-related legislation in the one hundredth United States Congress (in session from 6 January 1987 through 22 October 1988) showed that most of the 535 members did not vote on language issues in any consistent pattern outside of very broad liberal or conservative predilections regarding the role of government in public life; nevertheless, regional loyalties to various language groups, some indigenous, some immigrant, were clearly evident in the kinds of support given to various legislation pieces such as maintenance of indigenous languages, favored by most Western members of Congress regardless of party affiliation (Judd 1989).

In educational practice, some of the decision points related to language in education have become explicit (and controversial) when subjected to legislative action; bilingual education is the main case in point. However, many more are resolved through the thousands of everyday decisions made by individuals in local, state, and federal agencies and institutions who determine the kinds of services to provide in languages other than English; whether to provide other language support through oral assistance, written materials, or both; when to call for interpreters (and who constitutes an appropriate interpreter or translator); and how much time to devote to identifying and resolving language-related issues (Cloonan and Strine 1991; Ruiz 1994).

Ideological and structural tensions

Recent discussions of language planning emphasize the inadequacy of the rationalist, liberal beliefs that have, until now, shaped most of the public efforts to regulate language in the USA and elsewhere (Williams 1992; Phillipson 1992; Tollefson 1991; Luke et al. 1990). These commentators hold that, in applying positivist tenets of social science to matters of language use, scholars have overemphasized a rational, consensual approach to linguistic concerns and essentially ignored the power and validity of moral and emotional dimensions of language use and language regulation. Their concerns echo critics of the policy sciences in general, who suggest that the division between facts and values, a staple of rationalist analysis, is both spurious and simplistic. Because the political process is driven by questions of value, it is imperative that those be recognized and negotiated openly in a truly pluralist society (Hawkesworth 1988).

The tendency to impose a technical approach to problems that are not solely technical has been linked with the rhetoric of modernization. While this kind of rhetoric has not usually been applied to the English-speaking democracies (thought to be "modern" already), it is apparent in their past approaches to English language education for immigrants. To be a good American (or Australian, or Canadian), one had to learn English (McGroarty 1985; Singh 1992) and also, by implication, abandon pre-existing allegiances and attachments to other languages and cultures. Language use and language loyalty were, thus, conceived of in all-or-nothing terms, which excluded possibilities for public support of bilingualism and biculturalism. The necessity for English was presented as part of the drive for "equal opportunity and individual excellence", which has, to one degree or another, animated Western liberal democracies (Williams 1992:136). This emphasis on individual opportunity, coupled with a contemporary emphasis on the spheres of work or education as the appropriate domains for achievement, has meant a concurrent disinclination to deal with language use in any but individual terms. The possibility that a language or culture other than English could co-exist, even flourish, within the boundaries of the Anglophone democracies has not been entertained by commentators outside of minority language communities until recently (Wiley 1996).

In the USA, ideological positions based on the perspective of the dominant society have determined government education and language-in-education policies. Even the Chicago Progressives (including John Dewey and Jane Addams, who reacted against the dogmatic pronouncements of the Americanizers in the early part of this century) emphasized an ideal of American unity that incorporated newcomers through their acceptance of American values, beliefs, and behaviors; only gradually, and then incompletely, did they come to understand the persistence of ethnic identity (Lissak 1989:136). It is only with the growing numbers and political power of members of language minority communities themselves that alternatives to the rhetoric of complete assimilation, linguistic and otherwise, have been articulated.[5]

[5] The matter of which groups qualify as 'language-minority communities' is by no means straightforward. Some revisionist critiques of language policy reify minority communities into entities with a single purpose and unified position on language issues. It is vital to note that the members of other language communities differ amongst themselves with respect to their continued use of, attachments to, and beliefs about the value of languages and cultures other than the Anglophone; it is

On the contemporary American scene, frequent contacts between speakers of English and speakers of other languages have brought matters of language use into central focus, raising concerns about relationships between individual and group rights and institutional responsibilities. Where monolingual Americans have frequent contact with speakers of other languages, they often perceive language diversity as a problem. When linguistic diversity is linked to individual freedoms, the discourse has assumed the tenor of language-as-right, since this is a pillar of the individualism deeply enshrined in American national values (Spindler and Spindler 1990; Triandis 1990; Glendon 1991). Only sporadically has mainstream American society taken the position that language diversity is a resource (Ruiz 1984); this is done generally to justify better language education for monolingual speakers of English rather than to encourage the retention and development of bilingualism in indigenous or immigrant groups (Campbell and Schnell 1987). Indeed, most public discourse and legislative or executive decisions related to language have not been driven by appeals to ideals such as multilingualism or abstract beliefs regarding the place of multiple language abilities in a demanding academic curriculum. While these benefits may be adduced as secondary benefits, pragmatic and instrumental concerns that treat language learning as the means to other socially approved ends such as better educational attainment and enhanced job possibilities on the individual level or improved national security in the domains of trade, defense, or diplomacy at the national level, testify to Americans' pragmatic, and largely individualistic, orientations toward language issues.

---

dangerous to assume less intra-group variation in minority-language communities than in other communities of speakers, in the absence of actual evidence of greater consensus.

Relative size and number of language communities are also relevant to policy decisions in this connection. Moreover, the extent to which group members see themselves as a distinctive group and accept language as a core value of their culture (Smolicz 1980) determines the strength of community support for continued use of other languages in addition to that which is socially, if not numerically, dominant. Research with indigenous language groups suggests that acceptance of education in a minority language depends on both community attitudes regarding the appropriateness and goals of education and willingness to bring a minority language into new domains of use (D. McLaughlin 1992; Hornberger 1987), both factors that admit a wide range of behavioral responses.

Bilingual education: new federal–local connections

The education of children during the entire period they are legally required to attend school, usually between ages 5–16 (each of the 50 states sets its own legal school-leaving age), is a responsibility borne by local educational authorities in the form of elected school boards. Public education at these levels is financed through the system of state and local taxes, typically on real property, income, sales, or some combination of these. Each state has its own educational culture, reflecting its history and the patterns of leadership and influence emerging therein (Marshall et al. 1989). Hence each state's educational culture mirrors other aspects of state leadership, typically varying on such dimensions as the influence of elective versus appointed leaders; tensions between urban and rural areas within states; differing perspectives regarding issues of individual choice versus collective responsibilities in provision of schooling; and appropriate ways to garner and spend state revenues on education. The localism that reigns in education in general extends to procedures for identifying and serving students whose home language is not English. Each state has its own set of criteria, for the federal government requires that states have a procedure in place but does not specify what it should be (Olsen 1989).[6]

Given this diversity, it is surprising that there should be any uniformity at all in educational practice related to programs for students who do not speak English. Surprising, that is, until the federal role in education emerging from the Great Society programs of the 1960s and 1970s is taken into account. The legacy of the Great Society programs created a structure giving federal agencies a signal role in oversight of services for students whose native language is not English, mainly through tying provision of services to Civil Rights issues (Crawford 1989). Contemporary bilingual legislation, beginning with the 1968 Title VII of

---

[6] Not only the nature of appropriate criteria but the extent of their application to different groups of students have recently come under criticism in some large school districts, where it is thought that English-speaking children are being misplaced into bilingual education programs because of too rigid selection standards applied without regard to individual circumstances (Berger 1993). Such students then presumably displace others who need special language services. The extent and effects of this perceived phenomenon merit further careful study, particularly since it is known that federally funded bilingual programs serve less than 15 per cent of students identified as limited in English-speaking ability by whatever measure their respective states use.

the *Elementary and Secondary Education Act*, made federal dollars available on a competitive basis to school districts in which large numbers of students did not have English as a native language. Judicial pressures, ultimately embodied in the 1974 Lau vs Nichols decision, required school districts to provide special services to non-native speakers, though the form of the services was left vague.

Although supervision and enforcement of the regulations related to bilingual education fell off considerably during the Reagan–Bush years, as did the appropriations made available for it (Lyons 1990:74), many school districts developed arrangements for transitional bilingual programs. These typically lasted two to three years and required initial literacy instruction and native language support while students developed the English skills needed in mainstream classes. Enrollment pressures in many districts dictated more explicit attention to the instructional needs of non-native speakers, for their numbers grew rapidly during the 1970s and 1980s, particularly in large urban districts and in the Sunbelt. Additionally, more recent federal efforts in the areas of early childhood education have encouraged the development of high levels of English mastery even prior to Kindergarten entrance through so-called "developmental preschools" where English immersion was the rule. Advocates of bilingual instruction saw this as yet another example of the federal desire to stamp out other languages in the hope that, if all children spoke English before school entry, bilingual education at the K–12 level would become moot (Wong Fillmore 1991a; 1991b). Advocates further hold that both demographic trends and growing awareness of the length of time needed to master a language for academic purposes (Collier 1989; 1992) signal the continued relevance of bilingual instruction, even though it has been available to less than 15 per cent of the qualified student population.

Even on the face of it, though, the question about possible misplacement demonstrates the difficulties of basing all-or-nothing program placement decisions (students have access either to a bilingual program taught in Spanish or an all-English classroom; there are no other alternatives available) on a few simple questions about language background. As scholars and experienced educators have held for some time, the issue of linguistic competencies is far more complex than can be captured by surveys, questionnaires, or tests geared to dichotomous program decisions rather than description of a range of competencies in one, two, or more languages(Valdés and Figueroa 1994). For this reason, interest in alternative forms of language assessment continues to grow (cf. Wilkinson and Silliman 1990; Hamayan 1995)).

Using any amount of native language proved and still proves controversial (Crawford 1992a; 1992b). Polling a nationwide sample of
Americans about their attitudes toward bilingual education, political
scientists Huddy and Sears found that bilingual education was a highly
symbolic issue. Furthermore, strength of support among mainstream
non-minority respondents declined when bilingual education was
described as a means of maintaining a non-English mother tongue; in
contrast, it increased when it was described as a way to assist students
with development of English and academic skills (Sears and Huddy
1987; 1989). Proponents of the English-Only movement, a coalition of
private lobbying groups that grew up largely outside the education
establishment, have seized on the provision of federal monies for services in other languages as evidence of undue influence by speakers of
other languages on public services and called for its immediate demise
(Crawford 1992a; 1989:52–69)[7].

In the United States, bilingual education has generated public support
outside the ethnic communities it serves when defined as instrumental
in achieving a core American value—individual academic success. More
sophisticated advocates also promote the increased cognitive flexibility
that accompanies strong bilingual skills; this, too, is an individual factor.
The maintenance of non-English languages, though, has not found
much support outside of ethnic communities, although for many parents who themselves speak other languages, this is a paramount goal of
bilingual instruction. Certainly the cultural component of bilingual
instruction is often the core of the various forms of bilingual programs

---

[7] The English-Only movement has generated a barrage of commentary in professional and lay circles both; a number of current volumes and anthologies of articles on
the topic are available (eg, Adams and Brink 1990; Baron 1990; Cazden and Snow
1990; Crawford 1992a,b; Fishman 1988, to name just a few; and other articles listed in Carlisle 1992). Both the English-Only movement and its countervailing coalition, English Plus, represent the influence of articulate if relatively small interest
groups on local and national political agendas.

The centerpiece of the English-Only agenda, a constitutional amendment making
English the official language of the United States, has not yet passed Congress.
However, similar legislation with varying degrees of force has indeed been accepted in 17 states, though it was declared unconstitutional in one, Arizona (Common
Cause 1993, p. 6). Language professionals and other interested observers must thus
stay in touch with advocacy organizations and Congressional offices to discover the
eventual fate of national language legislation.

for American Indian groups (Crawford 1989). For many language minority groups, school instruction in the home language is not simply a linguistic means to the ultimate end of all-English schooling, but testimony to the enduring value and relevance of the home language and culture. Achievement of proficiency in two languages is, thus, only part of the motivation for supporting bilingual education programs within some language minority ethnic communities; promoting and maintaining a bicultural identity is another vital goal.

Conflict over the legitimacy of this goal (as well as serious practical and pedagogical questions about how best to achieve it) has continued to shape public debate (McGroarty 1992). It has, in addition, led to a virtual explosion of evaluations of bilingual education. The sheer numbers of evaluation studies demonstrate not only the use of program evaluation as a political tool, but also differing perspectives on what constitutes success in bilingual programs: skills in English are always assessed; skills in academic subjects sometimes measured; skills in languages other than English rarely recorded, and even less often analyzed (Cziko 1992); and cultural and social psychological outcomes rarely studied in depth, though these have been included more frequently within the last 10 years (cf. Cabazon et al. 1993). Program evaluation, particularly when conducted by federal agencies, has reflected the interest of the dominant society in the rapid learning of English, with relatively less emphasis on skill development in other academic areas and less still on cultural or attitudinal outcomes. However, the most recent large-scale evaluation of bilingual programs (Ramirez 1992) examines outcomes in such crucial areas as mathematics with much greater precision[8].

---

[8] The recent SRA Technologies evaluation study of three approaches to language minority education completed under US Department of Education sponsorship exceeded all its predecessors in collecting and analyzing pertinent data on skills in both English and, where appropriate, Spanish, the minority language at issue (see Ramirez, J. D. 1992; and other articles in the same issue of the *Bilingual Research Journal*). In demonstrating that the programs in which the use of Spanish for academic instruction was most intensive were the most successful in supporting student achievement across all subject areas, the study has given renewed support to proponents of native language instruction; for that reason, it has proven controversial as well, as indicated by the Bush Administration's efforts to convene a scientific panel to critique the study's methodology, already vetted through the usual consultative processes, once more prior to allowing release of results (Miller 1990).

Bilingualism for all: moves toward the mainstream

Many educators and members of the American public have been favorably inclined toward bilingual education when they see it as a more efficient means of learning English and mastering academic content. In many discussions, concern for these goals has overshadowed interest in achieving full bilingualism. Full bilingualism did not initially attract widespread mainstream support, but another pronouncement of the cyclical lamentations regarding Americans' linguistic ineptitude, the report of the President's Commission in 1979, led to renewed interest in providing programs that would help English speakers develop skills in other languages even as children who did not speak English learned it. Some program designers have sought to use the native speakers of other languages, where they exist in sufficient numbers, as resources to participate in two-way bilingual programs. Such programs, implemented mainly in Spanish in select locations around the country, are not yet widespread. Like other forms of bilingual instruction, they appear to yield optimal results when consistently implemented over an entire elementary school curriculum with well-trained teachers. Whether or not they become more widespread depends in part on how much effort the majority voters who elect school boards are willing to devote to producing a "language competent America" (Tucker 1991). Local and regional diversity in the salience of other language skills suggests that two-way programs will have a future in some parts of the country if they can successfully impart strong dual-language skills to students from language minority and mainstream communities. Yet, again, in these programs the linguistic goals are only part of overall program aims, which include providing students with greater knowledge of and ability to deal effectively with cultural differences. A recent study of a two-way developmental bilingual program in a Washington, DC, suburb indicated that many parents wanted children to participate to gain experience with a more diverse group of student peers (Craig 1994). Thus, many parents, even those who are not themselves bilingual, see two-way programs as a forum for developing the social as well as linguistic skills required in a multicultural future.

The growing institutionalization of bilingual education is almost unremarked as public debates regarding optimal forms and the ultimate worth of bilingual education continue (McGroarty 1992:9). Many states in the USA now offer or require special certification or endorsement for bilingual or ESL teachers. Of the 50 states, 29 make provision for special bilingual licensure and 36 offer a certificate or endorsement in English-as-a-second-language (ESL) instruction (McFarren et al. 1988; TESOL 1989). Generally, states that offer one also offer the other, a testimony to the recognition that both kinds of services have a place in the education of non-English-speaking students. The validity of bilingual instruction as well as ESL in a sound educational program for non-native speakers is further specified in the most recent policy document of the Teachers of English to Speakers of Other Languages (TESOL 1992). In addition, bilingual education has been endorsed by the largest mainstream teachers' organizations in the USA, the National Education Association (NEA), which first endorsed bilingual education in 1981 and amended the resolution in 1989; and the American Federation of Teachers (AFT), which adopted a supportive resolution in 1990[9]. Together, these organizations represent more than two million educators. Organizations for administrators have also shown interest, though they have taken no official position: the Association of Supervision and Curriculum Development (ASCD), which numbers about 150 000 members, has published an information document aimed at describing bilingual education, which implies support (ASCD 1987); Phi Delta Kappa, another administrative organization with a membership of approximately 132 000, has published two compilations of articles on the subject—one a relatively neutral collection of descriptive articles, the other an extended critique of bilingual education by a disenchanted bureaucrat. The National Council of Teachers of English (NCTE), a group one might expect to welcome English-Only initiatives, has emphatically rejected the idea that exclusive use of English is essential to educational success (Daniels 1990), as has the NEA (NEA 1988). All three national professional associations directly concerned with linguistics and English language teaching, the Linguistic Society of America (LSA), the American Association of Applied Linguistics (AAAL), and Teachers of English to Speakers of Other Languages (TESOL), passed resolutions opposing English Only and affirming linguistic diversity in 1995–96.

The issues surrounding bilingual education are perhaps the clearest indications of the conflicts in American language-in-education policies, conflicts driven by ideological differences regarding the value of bilingualism and structural tensions between different levels of educational

---

[9] Information on membership of these organizations and their positions on bilingual education obtained by phone from their national research or administrative offices between July and October 1990.

governance and between majority and minority groups. The federal government plays a role in requiring special language services for pupils who do not use English as a native language, but the amount of money appropriated is quite limited when compared to the numbers of students who qualify for services by any of the various definitions used throughout the states. Responsibilities for providing direct educational services fall on local educational agencies, which may or may not include personnel trained to provide either bilingual or ESL instruction. For American voters outside of professional education circles, bilingual education has taken on a symbolic value not directly tied to instructional issues but rather to attitudes about the federal government's role in regulating local practices, fiscal responsibility, and the desirability of recent immigrant groups. It is this symbolic level that proponents of English-only legislation and practice seek to exploit in claiming, lack of evidence notwithstanding, that English is under threat from the use of other languages and that by making the use of English mandatory, people will learn it faster.

Yet changing linguistic ideologies and the growing political influence of language minority groups have renewed public interest in the reality of bilingualism on the contemporary American scene. Increasingly, school districts where there are many non-native English-speaking students have implemented special programs. Where there are regional loyalties and sufficiently large numbers of language minority speakers, school programs may incorporate other languages and seek to develop and maintain bilingual skills for majority-language as well as minority-language students. Organizations of professional educators, increasingly cognizant of the numbers of students involved and the potential value of bilingual approaches, have demonstrated interest in and sometimes active endorsement of bilingual instruction. The overlapping and competing pressures from all these groups, as well as the tradition and legal structures establishing local governance in education, mean that diverse program designs and lively debate will be part of the American scene for some time to come.

Instruction in other languages: lofty visions, local realities

What has transpired in foreign language education for monolingual Americans during the past 25 years, as bilingual education has become better established? There has again arisen some interest in providing foreign language at the elementary level based on the powerful but inaccurate belief that younger children invariably learn languages faster than older students (McLaughlin, B. 1992). Some state boards have passed mandates requiring school districts to provide such instruction, but these are rarely accompanied by funds to train teachers or efforts to restructure the entire school curriculum to make additional instruction time available for this purpose. Still, in some areas of the country where there are sizeable communities using a non-English language such as Spanish, Chinese, or Navajo on a daily basis, local educators and school boards have worked energetically to develop programs in these languages aimed at giving elementary students some level of language proficiency and related cultural knowledge.

At the same time, though, many universities have dropped foreign language study as a requirement for entrance, thus reducing pressures on secondary schools to provide language instruction; in only 20 out of 37 states whose supervisors responded to a recent survey did more than 30 per cent of high school students take any foreign language classes (Draper 1991:4). The growing political and economic importance of certain members of other language groups, notably Spanish speakers, have attracted high school students to study this language in ever greater numbers, even as enrollments in French and German, the other two members of the perennial "big three" in American foreign language instruction, have declined. Yet, at the secondary level in particular, local initiatives have also led to implementation of such current and strategic languages as Arabic, Chinese, Japanese, and Russian (Draper 1991), depending on the availability of instructors and technological resources.

No state requires specified levels of foreign language proficiency to graduate from high school, although the current popularity of the ACTFL Proficiency Guidelines, revised to reflect the reality of high school instruction, attests to the desire of foreign language educators for some clear descriptions of what secondary level language students can do. If monolingual English-speaking students have the chance to study a non-English language, the two-year pattern noted as typical ever since the 1930s (Coleman 1934:4) is still likely to be the norm. Foreign language instruction, then, even more than bilingual education at the elementary level, reflects the diversity in approach and emphasis that is a logical result of highly localized governance patterns coupled with the greatly varying commitments and capabilities of local school districts to provide foreign language instruction throughout a student's secondary school career.

Post-secondary and tertiary institutions show greater uniformity in requirements with greater diversity in offerings. It is possible to get a Bachelor degree without any foreign language study. Three-quarters of two-year institutions have no language requirement, although 75 per cent of comprehensive universities and 90 per cent of Doctorate-granting institutions have one (Huber 1992). No college or university requires more than a two-year course of study; a distinct minority require demonstrated proficiency rather than completion of credit hours. Many college and university students now elect foreign language study as part of an overall career orientation. The growing awareness of the changing international economic and political scene has created considerable demand for instruction in Japanese, for example, since many students see this as a valuable occupational skill. Moreover, many students see mastery of Spanish as useful for work in the domestic as well as the international economy, so enrollments in Spanish have remained robust. At the postgraduate level, the number of programs linking language study to international business has grown considerably, not because of any major shift in American government policy decision but because the world of business is changing, becoming more international and less dominated by American interests. New trade agreements such as the North American Free Trade Agreement (NAFTA) may indeed encourage more widespread language study (Tucker 1993). Some of the more recent second language programs represent new links between entrepreneurial interests and the older area-studies tradition in American higher education (NCFLIS 1985), links forged at individual institutions with some federal support but not solely or even mainly because of federal initiative.

Delivery systems for occupational language training outside of institutions of higher education are even more fragmented (McGroarty 1993). This is, in part, due to the piecemeal nature of systems of post-secondary occupational training in general (Grubb and McDonnell 1991), and in part due to the existence of a network of private language schools, the extent and effectiveness of which is nearly impossible to gauge since no national statistics are kept (Lambert 1989). The federal government maintains its own training institutions for adult students in diplomatic service and the military. Employers, public or private, may provide short-term courses of instruction for employees who need to improve their skills in English or develop skills in other languages. There is no legal mandate that they do so, however, and consequently no mechanism for government-enforced language instruction exists. The right of an employee to use a language other than English on the job or to continue doing a job despite use of accented English has been challenged, sometimes protected and sometimes set aside by government action depending on the circumstances of particular cases (Piatt 1993). Where language rights have been enforced, they have been justified on the basis of an individual's right to do his or her job—note again the prevalence of individualism and the economic motive in rationalizing legal decisions. Policies related to post-secondary language education, unlike those governing elementary and secondary education, show a strong free market orientation in two senses: first, they show the value accorded institutional and individual choice in deciding which alternatives will be offered; and second, they reflect the reluctance or inability of federal and state government to provide extensive fiscal or pedagogical support for adult language training.

Some final thoughts

Over time, as majorities develop and coalesce around issues, as the number and influence of minority groups changes, and as the patterns of language maintenance within minority (and majority) language groups shift (Veltman 1983; 1988), so will the nature of public discussions and public policy related to language in the USA. It is, hence, unlikely that a unified and explicit American language policy will emerge in the proximate future. There is no doubt that English remains the dominant, even hegemonic, national language. Nevertheless, growing demographic diversity supports the continued vitality of other languages in the USA, with great local and regional variation the norm. American legal precedents protect some language rights and connect freedom to learn or use language to other individual freedoms. The federal union that respects a degree of local autonomy in providing language services allows local authorities, whether educational or in other institutions, to provide the special language services they see as justified (Cloonan and Strine 1991; McGroarty 1996).

Proponents of less government regulation, particularly those opposed to the use of languages other than English, decry this. Members of language minority groups, especially those groups not numerous enough to warrant linguistic adaptations or politically powerful enough to lobby for it, also take issue with such an approach, pointing out that excessive reliance on majoritarianism precludes consideration of theoretical equity for members of all language minority groups. Some scholars have indicated that it is indeed possible to develop models for differential treatment of languages in education and social services, in which speakers of widely used languages would, in effect, subsidize services for members of smaller groups (Pool 1991). However, given American reluctance to regulate individual behavior (and the present extreme reluctance to introduce new systems of taxation for services that not all Americans would find equally valuable), it is very unlikely that major national initiatives or reforms in the areas of language education will emerge any time soon. Support for complete functional bilingualism is not uniformly distributed across the country as a whole[10]. Nonetheless, in some geographic areas where bilingual skills are perceived as important, ambitious programs that put linguistic and cultural pluralism into practice through changes in curricular content and language have already become established.

Springing from the pressures brought to bear by activist members of language minority groups who can tap majority support, often by linking language-in-education policies to core American values such as individual achievement or economic advancement, the issues raised in this discussion suggest a distinctive role for language professionals and professional organizations in language policy-making. Language professionals can, as individuals and as members of organizations, press for an inclusive approach to policy-making where members of language minority and majority communities as well as language educators have a voice in local, state, and national decisions. Can language educators be spokespersons for the communities they serve? This issue demands discretion on the part of teachers, I believe. Growing awareness of the multiple perspectives in any community has led to an increasing number

---

[10] In some areas of the country where speakers of languages other than English constitute an absolute or near majority, their influence and the practical necessity of government and business institutions to communicate with all citizens has acted as a counter to the language restrictionist policies manifested in English-Only legislation and lobbying efforts. A recent example is the overturning of the English-Only county ordinance in Miami, Florida, testimony not only to the numerical power of Spanish speakers in Dade County but to recognition of Miami's role as a center of commercial and tourist activity in the Spanish-speaking Americas (Rohter 1993).

who argue that teachers should not presume to speak on behalf of language minority communities unless they themselves are members of the group. Still, teachers may sometimes be closer and more knowledgeable about the experiences of language minority students than other members of the dominant group; in such cases, they can (and often must) serve as community advocates while respecting the legitimacy of the various positions within any language community regarding language maintenance, teaching, and use. As trained professionals, language educators can provide current, accurate, and accessible information on how languages are best learned and taught, can share this with interested parties, and can help to articulate policy alternatives appropriate to local circumstances. Through their professional organizations, they can produce statements of principle regarding the need to respect all languages and language varieties, the legitimacy of all varieties to serve as vehicles for instruction in different circumstances, and the importance of multiple language models and optimal program designs, including participatory curriculum design and comprehensive and innovative evaluation standards (Wiley 1996).

But information and analysis are not sufficient to guarantee good policies in language or in any other sphere of activity. In the political sphere, adequate data on various alternative courses of action are rarely available prior to all decision points (Rist 1994). Furthermore, as Weiss remarks, "What actually happens depends on the mix of interests, ideologies, and institutional procedures in the political domain and on the political will to make things happen" (1992:13–14). To affect language education policies in the USA, language educators must be willing to help create a climate of opinion favorable to provision of good language services and an environment where political will and the required resources can be directed toward this goal through available electoral and representative processes. They can seek to influence politicians through provision of timely, specific, and informed critiques of possible alternatives; they can and should articulate the myths and facts surrounding the symbolic aspects of language teaching and use and be willing to recognize and address the emotional valence of popular beliefs about language and language learning. Such principles and courses of action, best summed up as informed advocacy, accord with American values, mores, and legal precedents. In the USA, language professionals are one, but only one, of the many groups that have a legitimate stake in language education. Commitment to a truly pluralist vision requires recognition of this socio-historical context and a willingness to engage in the constant processes of negotiation, overt and implicit, that govern American educational practice.

References

Adams, K. and Brink, D. (eds) 1990 *Perspectives on Official English*. New York: Mouton de Gruyter.

Association for Supervision and Curriculum Development (ASCD) 1987 *Building an Indivisible Nation: Bilingual Education in Context*. Alexandria, VA: Author.

Baldauf, R. B., Jr. 1994 'Unplanned' language policy and planning. In W. Grabe et al. (eds) Annual Review of Applied Linguistics 1993–1994. New York: Cambridge University Press. 82–89.

Baron, D. 1990 *The English-Only Question*. New Haven: Yale University Press.

Berger, J. 4 January 1993 *New York's bilingual bureaucracy assailed as non-English programs cover more pupils*. New York Times. A13.

Cabazon, M., Lambert, W. and Hall, G. 1993 *Two-way Bilingual Education: A Progress Report on the Amigos Program*. Research report no. 7. Santa Cruz, CA: National Center for Research on Cultural Diversity and Second Language Learning, University of California.

Campbell, R. and Schnell, S. 1987 *Language conservation*. Annals of the American Academy of Political and Social Science 490. 177–85.

Carlisle, R. March 1992 *Official English and Bilingual Education: A Bibliography*. Vancouver, BC: Paper presented at the 26th TESOL Convention.

Cazden, C., and Snow, C. (eds) 1990 English plus: issues in bilingual education. Special issue of *Annals of the American Academy of Political and Social Science 508*.

Cloonan, J. D. and Strine, J. M. 1991 Federalism and the development of language policy: preliminary investigations. *Language Problems and Language Planning 15.3*. 268–81.

Coleman, A. 1934 *Experiments and Studies in Modern Language Teaching*. Chicago, IL: University of Chicago Press.

Collier, V. 1989 How long? A synthesis of research on academic achievement in a second language. *TESOL Quarterly 23.3*. 509–31.

Collier, V. 1992 A synthesis of studies examining long-term language minority student data on academic achievement. *Bilingual Research Journal* (formerly *NABE Journal*) 16.1/2. 187–212.

Common Cause. January 1993 English as the Official Language of the United States. State issue brief. Washington, DC: Author.

Cooper, R. L. 1989 *Language Planning and Social Change*. Cambridge: Cambridge University Press.

Craig, B. 1994 *American Attitudes toward Bilingualism: Implications for Language Acquisition Planning.* Paper presented at the American Association for Applied Linguistics Conference in March, Baltimore, MD.

Crawford, J. 1989 *Bilingual Education: History, Politics, Theory, and Practice.* Trenton, NJ: Crane Publishing.

Crawford, J. 1992a *Hold Your Tongue: Bilingualism and the Politics of 'English Only'.* Reading, MA: Addison-Wesley.

Crawford, J. (ed.) 1992b *Language Loyalties: A Source Book on the Official English Controversy.* Chicago, IL: University of Chicago Press.

Cziko, G. 1992 The evaluation of bilingual education. *Educational Researcher* 21.2. 10–15.

Daniels, H. A. (ed.) 1990 *Not Only English: Affirming America's Multilingual Heritage.* Urbana, IL: National Council of Teachers of English.

Draper, J. B. 1991 *Dreams, Realities, and Nightmares: The Present and Future of Foreign Language Education in the United States.* Report prepared for Joint National Committee for Languages in cooperation with the National Council of State Supervisors of Foreign Languages.

Fishman, J. (ed.) 1986 Special issue on English Only. *International Journal of the Sociology of Language 60.*

Glendon, M. A. 1991 *Rights Talk: The Impoverishment of Political Discourse.* New York: The Free Press.

Grubb, W. N. and McDonnell, L. M. July 1991 *Local Systems of Vocational Education and Job Training: Diversity, Interdependence, and Effectiveness.* Berkeley, CA: National Center for Research in Vocational Education.

Hamayan, E. V. 1995 Approaches to alternative assessment. *Annual Review of Applied Linguistics 15.* 212–226.

Hawkesworth, M. E. 1988 *Theoretical Issues in Policy Analysis.* Albany: State University of New York Press.

Heath, S. B. April 1988 American language policy in social historical perspective. In *Proceedings of the Conference on Language Rights and Public Policy.* Stanford, CA: Stanford University. 1–4.

Hornberger, N. H. 1987 Bilingual education success, but policy failure. *Language in Society 16.* 205–26.

Huber, B. J. Fall 1992 Enrollments in foreign languages. *ADFL Bulletin.* 12–14.

Judd, E. L. April 1989 *Language Policy and the 100th Congress.* Paper presented at the 23rd TESOL Convention, San Antonio, TX.

Kloss, H. 1977 *The American Bilingual Tradition.* Rowley, MA: Newbury House.

Lambert, R. D. 1989 The National Foreign Language System. Occasional Paper no. 6. Washington, DC: National Foreign Language Center at Johns Hopkins University.

Leibowitz, A. H. 1982 *Federal Recognition of the Rights of Minority Language Groups.* Rosslyn, VA: National Clearinghouse for Bilingual Education.

Lissak, R. S. 1989 *Pluralism and Progressives: Hull House and the New Immigrants, 1890–1919.* Chicago, IL: University of Chicago Press.

Luke, A., McHoul, A. W. and Mey, J. L. 1990 On the limits of language planning: class, state, and power. In R. B. Baldauf, Jr., and A. Luke (eds) *Language Planning and Education in Australasia and the South Pacific.* Clevedon, England: Multilingual Matters. 25–44.

Lyons, J. J. 1990 *The past and future directions of federal bilingual-education policy.* Annals of the American Academy of Political and Social Science 508. 66–80.

McFerren, M., Valadez, C. M., Crandall, J., Palomo, R. S. and Gregoire, C. P. 1988 *Certification of Language Educators in the United States. Educational report no. 11.* Los Angeles, CA: Center for Language Education and Research (CLEAR), University of California, Los Angeles. (ED 291–243).

McGroarty, M. 1985 From citizen to consumer: images of the learner in adult ESL texts. *Issues in Education 3.* 13–30.

McGroarty, M. 1992 The societal context of bilingual education. *Educational Researcher 21.2.* 7–9, 24.

McGroarty, M. 1993 Second language instruction in the workplace. In *Annual Review of Applied Linguistics 13.* New York: Cambridge University Press. 86–108.

McGroarty, M. 1996 *Multilingualism in the U. S. federal system: equity or expediency?* Paper presented at the American Association of Applied Linguistics (AAAL) Conference, Chicago, IL, March.

McLaughlin, B. 1992 *Myths and Misconceptions about Second Language Learning: What Every Teacher Needs to Unlearn. Educational practice report no. 5.* Santa Cruz, CA: National Center for Research on Cultural Diversity and Second Language Learning, University of California.

McLaughlin, D. 1992 *When Literacy Empowers: Navajo Language in Print.* Albuquerque: University of New Mexico Press.

Marshall, C., Mitchell, D. and Wirt, F. 1989 *Culture and Education Policy in the American States.* New York: Falmer Press.

Miller, J. A. 31 October 1990 Native-language instruction found to aid L.E.P.'s: E.D. study may bolster case for bilingual ed. *Education Week.* 1, 23.

National Center for Education Statistics (NCES) June 1992 Public elementary and secondary school agencies in the US and outlying areas: school year 1990–91. Washington, DC: Author. American Statistical Index fiche 4834–17; ASI 1991.

National Council for Foreign Language Education and International Studies (NCFLIS) 1985 *The Training of, and US Business' Needs for, International Specialists.* Conference proceedings. University of Massachusetts at Amherst.

National Education Association (NEA) April 1988 *Official English/English Only: More Than Meets the Eye.* Washington, DC: Author.

National Education Association (NEA) 1990 *Federal Education Funding: The Cost of Excellence.* Washington, DC: Author.

Olsen, R. W.-B. 1989 A survey of limited English proficient student enrollments and identification criteria. *TESOL Quarterly 23.* 469–88.

Phillipson, R. 1992 *Linguistic Imperialism*. Oxford: Oxford University Press.

Piatt, B. 1990 *Only English? Law and Language Policy in the United States.* Albuquerque: University of New Mexico Press.

Piatt, B. 1993 *Language on the Job: Balancing Business Needs and Employee Rights.* Albuquerque, NM: University of New Mexico Press.

Pool, J. 1991 The official language problem. *American Political Science Review* 85.2. 495–514.

Ramirez, J. D. 1992 Executive summary of final report: Longitudinal Study of Structured English Immersion Strategy, Early-Exit, and Late-Exit Transitional Bilingual Education programs for language-minority children. In *Bilingual Research Journal* (formerly *NABE Journal*) 16.1/2. 1–62.

Rist, R. 1994 Influencing the policy process with qualitative research. In N. Denzin and Y. Loncoln (eds) *Handbook of Qualitative Research*. Thousand Oaks, CA: Sage. 545–57.

Rohter, L. 14 May 1993 *Repeal is likely for 'English Only' policy in Miami*. New York Times. A7.

Ruiz, R. 1984 Orientations in language planning. *NABE Journal 7*. 15–34.

Ruiz, R. 1994 Language policy and planning in the US In W. Grabe et al. (eds) *Annual Review of Applied Linguistics 1993/1994.* New York: Cambridge University Press. 111–25.

Schlossman, S. L. 1983 Is there an American tradition of bilingual education? German in the public elementary schools, 1840–1919. *American Journal of Education, 91*. 139–186.

Sears, D. O. and Huddy, L. September 1987 Bilingual Education: Symbolic Meaning and Support among Non-Hispanics. Paper presented at meeting of the American Psychological Association, New York.

Sears, D. O. and Huddy, L. 1989 Language Conflict as Symbolic Politics: The Role of Symbolic Meaning. Unpublished ms. Los Angeles: University of California.

Singh, F. 1992 Teaching English to adult speakers of other languages, 1910–1920. *College ESL 2*. 44–53.

Smolicz, J. 1980 Language as a core value of culture. *RELC Journal 11*. 1–13.

Sonntag, S. K. and Pool, J. 1987 Linguistic denial and linguistic self-denial: American ideologies of language. *Language Problems and Language Planning 11.1.* 46–65.

Spindler, G. and Spindler, L. 1990 *The American Cultural Dialogue and Its Transmission*. London: Falmer Press.

Teachers of English to Speakers of Other Languages (TESOL). 24 October 1992 TESOL statement on the role of bilingual education in the education of children in the United States. Alexandria, VA: Author.

Tollefson, J. W. 1991 *Planning Language, Planning Inequality: Language Policy in the Community*. London: Longman.

Triandis, H. C. 1990 Theoretical concepts that are applicable to the study of ethnocentrism. In R. Brislin (ed.) *Applied Cross-Cultural Psychology*. Newbury Park, CA: Sage Publications. 34–55.

Tucker, G. R. 1991 Developing a language-competent American society: the role of language planning. In A. G. Reynolds (ed.) *Bilingualism, multiculturalism, and second language learning*. Hillsdale, NJ: Lawrence Erlbaum. 65–79.

Tucker, G. R. 1993 Language learning for the 21st century: challenges of the North American Free Trade Agreement. *Canadian Modern Language Review 50.1*. 165–72.

Valdés, G. and Figueroa, R. A. 1994 *Bilingualism and Testing: A Special Case of Bias*. Norwood, NJ: Ablex.

Veltman, C. 1983 *Language Maintenance and Shift in the US*. Berlin: Mouton.

Veltman, C. 1988 *The Future of the Spanish Language in the United States*. New York and Washington, DC: Hispanic Policy Development Project.

Weiss, C. 1992 Helping government think: functions and consequences of policy analysis organizations. In C. Weiss (ed.) *Organizations for Policy Analysis*. Newbury Park, CA: Sage Publications. 1–18.

Wiley, T. G. 1996 Language planning and policy. In S. L. McKay and N. H. Hornberger (eds) *Sociolinguistics and Language Teaching*. New York: Cambridge University Press. 103–147.

Wilkinson, L. C. and Silliman, E. 1990 Sociolinguistic analysis: nonformal assessment of children's language and literacy skills. *Linguistics and Education 2*. 109–25.

Williams, G. 1992 *Sociolinguistics: A Sociological Critique*. London: Routledge.

Wong Fillmore, L. 1991a A question for early-childhood programs: English first or families first? *Education Week 19* June 1991. 32, 34.

Wong Fillmore, L. 1991b When learning a second language means losing the first. *Early Childhood Research Quarterly 6*. 323–46.

CHAPTER 5

ENGLISH LANGUAGE-IN-EDUCATION POLICIES IN CANADA

Alister Cumming[11]
Modern Language Centre, Ontario Institute for Studies in Education,
Toronto, Canada

One must speak using plurals to describe Canada's language policies and language-in-education practices—and speak of pluralities. To call Canada an English-speaking country is appropriate only as an over-generalisation, applicable to just over two-thirds of the country's 25 million people.

Canada has two official languages, English and French, though the vast majority of the population uses only one of these languages routinely. The English-dominant and French-dominant populations are mostly located in different geographical areas, so societal situations of English/French bilingualism actually exist in just a few cities—Montreal, Ottawa, and Moncton—although legislation requires federal government services and information about commercial goods to be available in both languages, thus accommodating small numbers of Anglophones and Francophones who are also spread across the country. Moreover, numerous indigenous languages (in varying degrees of vitality) are used by First Nations peoples throughout the expanse of the country. And many families use languages in their homes and communities—such as Cantonese, Italian, Polish, Portuguese, or Punjabi—related to their ancestral heritages from other parts of the world.

Despite the complexities of these circumstances, the major policies and practices typical of English language in education in Canada can be sketched out by distinguishing three populations commonly learning

[11] I thank Barbara Burnaby, David Corson, Jean Handscombe, and Merrill Swain for their helpful comments on an initial draft of this paper.

English as a second language (ESL): recent immigrants and refugees in English-dominant Canada, Francophones in Québec, and First Nations peoples. Previous reviews of the ESL situation in Canada have highlighted these same populations (Allen and Swain 1984; Ashworth 1988; Burnaby 1987; Burnaby and Cumming 1992; Mallea 1989), but I will elaborate on additional documentary sources as well as personal impressions. Figure 6 outlines an overly overgeneralised overview— demarcated by policies, practices, and language maintenance conditions for school-age and for adult learners of English. Note that this figure ignores, only for the sake of brevity, the situations of five additional, distinct populations of learners of English in Canada: students from overseas studying at high schools, colleges or universities on short-term visas, mainly for academic purposes or educational travel (see Canadian Bureau for International Education 1981); native-born Canadian children entering school from families and communities using a language other than English at home (see Canadian School Trustees Association 1989 and Anderson 1918 for a historical perspective); persons settling in Canada who speak a variety of English as their dominant language that is perceived to have a different prestige from Canadian norms, particularly from the Caribbean, India, or Africa (see Coelho 1988; Corson 1994); Francophone communities in English-dominant settings outside of Québec (see Churchill 1986; Mougeon and Heller 1986); and non-Francophones in Québec learning English despite official policies promoting their acquisition of French (see d'Anglejan and De Koninck 1992; McAndrew 1993).

As Figure 6 indicates, no single, coherent policy addresses the variety of populations in Canada for whom English language in education is at issue; Canada may never wish or be able to adopt one. Rather, policies and practices for languages-in-education tend to be formulated in different ways for different groups and often so generally, if at all, that they may exist in fragile balance between regional interests, institutional practices, as well as societal conditions—subsuming or maintaining languages other than English or French, adapting to demographic changes, and responding to initiatives from all jurisdictions (Burnaby and Cumming 1992; Mallea 1989). Even the most specific of curriculum guidelines for English as a second language (ESL) education in Canadian schools (Ontario Ministry of Education 1988) is exceedingly (and necessarily) cautious in its classification of student populations and advice for instruction. Many other provinces simply have not been able to formulate or maintain curricula current for ESL education because of the fragility of interests and diversity of perspectives that would need to be brought to consensus.

Even if the goals of ESL policies have seldom been articulated precisely, the overall state of ESL education in Canada is hardly underdeveloped, or even gloomy. ESL education has experienced much activity in Canada over the past two decades, placing us in a favorable position internationally regarding such matters as teacher education, curriculum models, subsidised programs for adult learners, ESL literacy materials like learner newspapers (eg, Acosta 1981–present), bilingual education, antiracist education, and native language maintenance.

Obvious disjunctures—between policies, practices, and societal conditions—exist for immigrants and refugees learning English in Canada. Immigration is regulated federally, but two-thirds of all immigrants to Canada with little proficiency in English or French settle in or around only three cities: Toronto, Montreal, and Vancouver (Pendakur and Ledoux 1991). Public schooling and higher education are regulated and funded independently by each of Canada's ten provinces and two territories, but institutional policies for language education are mostly determined at the level of individual school board or educational institution. Moreover, private language schools and community agencies are assuming increased responsibilities for language education and immigrant settlement services. From 1991 to 1995, federal quotas for immigration have been raised to nearly double from previous years—in response to low birthrates, labour demands, and refugee migration throughout the world.

For the more than 50 000 adult immigrants or refugee claimants arriving annually in Canada with no proficiency in English, the federal government allocates funds to selected colleges, school boards, and private agencies for several months of full-time language instruction and orientation. Two such programs now exist nationally, replacing a variety of programs that operated in previous decades: Language Instruction for Newcomers to Canada (LINC) for basic language and literacy training and orientation to Canadian life; and Labour Market Language Training (LMLT) for language instruction at an intermediate level of proficiency linked to job preparation.

But the classes provided through these programs are scarcely able to meet the demands, despite recent government attempts to increase the number of adult learners receiving basic ESL instruction. For example, in British Columbia in 1991, only 19 per cent of adults studying ESL in that province were receiving such government funding; others were paying tuition fees themselves (at rates of between Can$1.00 and Can$6.60 per hour of instruction), and waiting lists to enter adult ESL courses were nearly as populous as the numbers of students attending such classes (Cumming 1991).

Immigrants/Refugees	Québecois(e)	First Nations
1. SCHOOL-AGE CHILDREN AND YOUTH		
Official Policies for ESL:		
—vary from explicit guidelines to none, by province, by school board, and by school, depending on extent of multilingual diversity	—standard curriculum for intermediate and secondary schools throughout province	—vary by province and band[12], depending on vitality of Aboriginal language and local priorities
Institutional Practices for ESL:		
—vary from no formal direction to withdrawal to language and content to mainstreaming —orientation and placement centres in some cities	—follow official curriculum despite extent of language contact	—vary from no formal direction to Whole Language adopted for local commercial programs, eg, Distar commercial
Maintenance of Languages Other Than English:		
—some heritage language programs of full- or part-time study in urban centres in schools or other institutions —anti-racist education —ethnic or religious associations —"modern languages" taught as subjects	—French promoted actively as single official language —some mother tongue main- tenance, eg, PELO, ethnic or religious associations	—vary from active promotion (eg, Inuit) as medium of instruction in initial schooling to L1 and culture as subjects of instruction to no treatment —anti-racist education

[12] Many schools for First Nations populations are organised by a local council of Aboriginal peoples, representing a self-defined autonomous jurisdiction who refer to themselves as a 'band' in many parts of Canada.

Immigrants/Refugees	Québecois(e)	First Nations

2. ADULTS

Official Policies for ESL:

Immigrants/Refugees	Québecois(e)	First Nations
—basic ESL and literacy (LINC) funded —intermediate ESL for work (LMLT) funded —programs sustained at colleges, school boards, private businesses, and immigrant-serving agencies —student visas for short-term study in higher education	—none	—none

Institutional Practices for ESL:

Immigrants/Refugees	Québecois(e)	First Nations
—intensive or part-time study at colleges, universities, private businesses, community or religious centres, or government-sponsored within agencies —some work-place —screening tests for credentials	—intensive or part-time study at colleges or private businesses —mainstreaming English universities and colleges higher education and	—support centres in universities and colleges —literacy and vocational upgrading —transition-year programs and literacy programs

Maintenance of Languages Other Than English:

Immigrants/Refugees	Québecois(e)	First Nations
—a few innovative programs in or for work, eg, Cantonese businesses —ethnic or religious associations —"modern languages" in higher education	—ethnic, religious, or community associations	—a few innovative programs for language revival

Figure 6
Current policies and practices for three populations learning English in educational settings in Canada

Over the past 20 years most colleges, community service agencies, and continuing education programs at universities and school boards in Canadian cities have established centres or programs for adults to study ESL. In colleges and universities, these ESL programs (for recent immigrants) often operate alongside EFL programs (for visiting students to Canada), whose higher tuition fees provide supplementary funding, resources, and bases for ongoing teacher employment. Typically, full-time and part-time courses are offered, operating on a cost-recovery basis (from federal government sources or student fees), but usually in isolation from programs of academic, vocational, or technical study. Indeed, at an institutional level, adult education policies have tended to be exclusionary rather than accommodating of immigrants to Canada. Institutions of higher education have mostly responded to increased populations with limited English by screening applicants through language proficiency tests prior to admissions (Elson 1992). Similarly, immigrants often find their entry into professions and trades in Canada blocked by language proficiency or certification requirements (Cumming, P. et al. 1989). Only a small number of businesses or industries employing workers with limited English have taken on responsibilities for language instruction in their workplaces, and even fewer have begun to address the complex curriculum issues entailed (Burnaby et al. 1992).

For immigrant children in English Canada, educational policies are much less uniform because (1) each province regulates its programs and funding for ESL independently, (2) the demographics of immigrant settlement vary dramatically throughout the country and are subject to annual changes, and (3) curricula, instructional policies, and resource allocations are mainly determined at the level of school district or individual school (Ashworth 1988; Canadian School Trustees' Association 1989; Cumming et al. 1993). Most urban school boards in immigrant-receiving areas have extensive ESL, orientation, community liaison, and academic integration programs, for example in the inner city centres of Toronto and Vancouver, where the majority of students now have home languages other than English. But funding and curricula differ markedly within districts and from school to school in such urban and suburban areas (Ashworth 1988; Cumming et al. 1993). In many new suburbs, smaller towns, rural areas, or cities in the Prairies and provinces on the Atlantic coast, where few immigrants settle, only limited ESL curricula and resources are available—often as withdrawal programs with part-time or itinerant staff. Local programming for ESL in Canada appears to follow a principle of critical mass, waiting for population growths to reach a level of about 10 per cent to 15 per cent limited-English speakers in local communities before formulating distinct educational and social policies (Cumming, A. 1991:142). At the same time, certain areas have seen remarkable growth in ESL populations; for example, Cumming, Hart, Corson and Cummins' (1993) analyses of census data between the years 1986 and 1991 show increases of between 40 per cent and 90 per cent in school-age students unable to speak either English or French in most areas of southern Ontario.

Francophone learners of English in Québec

For the six million Francophones residing in Québec, English is typically taught as a school subject, in effect as a "foreign" language (much as French is learned in most of English Canada). In the 1980s the provincial government introduced an extensive, innovative, standard curriculum for English studies, based on principles of communicative language teaching as well as considerable research and development (Ministere de l'Education, Gouvernement du Québec 1981 to 1986). Although presenting a distinct advance over previous audio-lingual teaching methods, English language curricula remain heavily regimented and centralised in Québec schools, overshadowed politically by active French-language maintenance throughout the province; increasing numbers of immigrant minorities, particularly in greater Montreal, perceived to require assimilation (into French, rather than English); and apprehension about the subtle encroachment of media and values from English Canada and the United States.

As a consequence, societal contacts tend to determine Québeckers' acquisition of English at least as much as schooling does. For example, many Francophones develop full English–French bilingualism if they are living in areas in ongoing contact with English, like Montreal or Hull, whereas residents of other parts of Québec may find their uses of English restricted to occasional travels or business contacts outside the province. Although no official policies exist for adult English instruction in Québec, the presence of several English-medium universities and colleges in Montreal provide opportunities for Francophones to register in academic or vocational programs, effectively mainstreaming themselves into the English milieu without sacrificing their native cultural environment. Moreover, many young adults in Québec pursue ESL courses at colleges, universities, or private language schools, or they sojourn in the USA or English Canada to learn English. Business contacts, vacations, and reading materials in English typically provide further opportunities for informal language contact and acquisition.

First Nations learners of English

The situations of the half-million First Nations peoples differ so greatly within Canada as to defy any generalisations about language-in-education policies. The theme of school failure has been prominent in studies of their education, considerably more so than for immigrant populations in Canada (Burnaby 1982; Mackay and Myles 1989). But the history of their conquest and assimilation, for example through "residential schools", has been one of the most shameful in Canada's history (Barman et al. 1986; Haig-Brown 1988). For many First Nations peoples, English-medium schooling represents the ambivalent functions of providing opportunities for education, work, and social advancement but also the main vehicle for cultural assimilation. Although most First Nations peoples learn English or French effectively at school and through social contacts, situations regarding the vitality of indigenous languages differ from extremes of morbidity, replaced by English as the language of home, school, and society (Burnaby and Beaujot 1986) to active promotion of a vernacular language, written script, and public media (Burnaby 1985)—such as Inuktitut among the Inuit of northern Québec or Cree in Northern Ontario or Manitoba—making it a viable basis for initial schooling followed by English in later grades (Burnaby 1982; Faries 1989). Despite the omnipresent political forces operating against school and societal achievement for First Nations populations (Ryan 1989), various initiatives have been attempted in past decades, focused mainly on bands assuming responsibilities for their local schools (see particularly Barman et al. 1987) but also including revitalisation efforts in several indigenous scripts and spoken languages, the creation of culturally appropriate materials for English instruction, local assessments of learning and curricular needs, and the formation of centres in institutions of higher education to support native learners (Barman et al. 1987; Burnaby 1982; Rodriguez and Sawyer 1990).

Prevalent issues and recent developments

For all three learner populations and both age groups discussed above, five broad issues impose limitations on current policies for English language education, yet at the same time represent areas of promising, recent developments.

1. Equity of access to language education

Disparities clearly exist in terms of who has access to what quality and extent of English language education in Canada. For example, nearly twice as many women as men are unable to speak either official language, an imbalance that evidently emerges *after* immigrants settle in Canada, given that gender distributions have long been equivalent among adults arriving in Canada with limited English or French (Boyd 1992; Cumming, A. 1991; Thomas 1990). Similarly, immigrant children in rural settings receive few of the educational opportunities for language education or language maintenance available in urban or suburban centres, which themselves differ considerably in relevant curricula and resources (Ashworth 1988). In response to such inequities, several analysts have advocated that education in one of Canada's official languages be considered as a fundamental human right for all Canadians requesting it (Burnaby and Cumming 1992). Current initiatives by the federal government are aimed at reducing some of these inequities for adult women, for example, by providing childcare, greater numbers of classes, transportation subsidies, etc. (Canada Employment and Immigration Advisory Council 1991; Immigration Canada 1991). And many urban school boards have implemented programs that accommodate the broadest range of learners and cultural backgrounds. But of course, even if universal provisions for language education were made available, countless difficulties would remain in determining eligibility, assuring appropriate educational conditions, and surmounting systemic barriers outside of educational settings. Moreover, regional differences and interests militate against a strongly centralised, national policy that might apply to all learner groups and local situations uniformly. And much ambivalence exists over recent initiatives that have imposed uniform curricula and policies for language education, in view of issues of local control and decision-making, such as LINC for adult immigrants or ESL in Québec schools.

2. Tensions between regional situations and differing levels of responsibility

To many people in Canada, the situation of English language policy seems like a political football, in which appeals for funding or development are tossed between local, regional, provincial, and federal responsibilities—with few means for coordination between agencies (Burnaby and Cumming 1992; Canadian School Trustees' Association 1989). This problem is exacerbated by the imbalanced demographic distribution of immigrant settlement and economic prosperity regionally in Canada, the long-standing separation of funding and policy mechanisms for the three populations described above, local fears of federal government intrusion into institutional or provincial policies, underfunding of educational programs, as well as the location of First Nations populations in scattered locations across the country. As a consequence, the persons with the greatest needs for language education tend to be in circumstances least readily addressed. For example, where does the adult refugee with limited English, limited vocational skills, *and* limited literacy fit in to current educational programs? To ESL, to literacy, or to job training programs? Sadly, the case is typically that none of these educational "solutions" are suitable, despite this profile matching a significant proportion of adult immigrants to Canada.

3. Relations of language education to other societal issues and cultural processes

The situations of populations learning English in Canada are, of course, closely interconnected with other political issues and cultural processes, such as literacy, academic achievement, social class, employment, and intergroup relations. Cognisant of these relations, many recent curriculum theories in Canada have developed bases for the integration of English language instruction with academic studies, work environments, and societal participation (eg, Mohan 1986), and many school policies have been established upon this premise (eg, Early and Hooper 1992; Ontario Ministry of Education 1988). Policies for adult education are now often phrased in reference to "participation in Canadian society" rather than the narrow, skill-based definitions of language proficiency emphasised only a decade ago. Moreover, awareness of the centrality of language education has also featured in an extraordinary number of recent commissioned reports and analyses on topics of broad societal interest, such as health care (Beiser et al. 1988), literacy (Jones 1992), employment (Pendakur 1992), racism (Lewis 1992), and aging (St Lawrence 1989). Nonetheless, many ESL programs remain structurally isolated from the very community, academic, or work environments for which learners strive to gain membership—an arrangement that may hinder rather than foster the socialisation processes desired (eg, Cumming and Gill 1991).

4. Maintenance of languages other than English or French

Conditions for maintenance of languages other than English are a point of considerable controversy in urban Canadian schools and news media, a controversy that has persisted throughout this century (eg, Anderson 1918). Minority-language children's acquisition of English is now simply inevitable in schools in Anglophone Canada, and virtually everywhere desired by teachers and families alike. Indeed, most languages other than English or French appear to be maintained only for two or three generations in Canada (Pendakur 1990). Efforts to promote children's home languages and long-term bilingualism have, however, been visibly resisted in many schools, despite research and advocacy arguing for the societal and personal benefits of maintaining minority languages as well as children's rights to schooling in their dominant language (Cummins 1984, 1989). School boards in some cities (eg, Toronto, Winnipeg, Edmonton) have established distinct policies to promote ethnic languages and cultures, and some provinces have developed curriculum guidelines, for example, for Heritage Languages in Ontario (Cummins 1984, 1989), and PELO (programme d'enseignement des langues d'origine) in Québec (McAndrew 1993; Painchaud 1993). But for the most part this educational function has been sustained only by community and religious organisations, usually on an informal or symbolic basis with limited resources and funding. In higher education, language curricula mainly remain as so-called "modern languages", taught as subjects related to the literatures or cultures of foreign nations, although increasing numbers of young adults use these courses to develop literacy in their ancestral, ethnic languages, such as Chinese, Italian, or Punjabi. Language maintenance situations have become especially visible in recent years as larger ethnic communities develop in Canadian cities and certain rural areas, fostered by an immigration policy that favours sponsorship by family members already residing in the country, available employment opportunities situated in certain regions, and the existence of social networks and services in certain languages capable of supporting immigrant settlement (Thomas 1990). Realisation of the broad, systemic basis of prejudices against ethnic languages and cultures in Canada has recently prompted the development of numerous anti-racist education programs for teachers, students and community workers (eg, Cumming and Mackay 1993; Cummins 1988; Ontario Ministry of Education and Training 1993).

5. Developing resources, research, theories, and facilitating structures

Despite Canada's long-standing interests in language policies, it is only in the past two decades that theories, research, and institutional bodies have really begun to address educational issues for immigrant, ethnic minority, or First Nations learners of English. Most studies of language issues in Canada have focused on the situations of majority (English or French) background learners of the two official languages. In educational practice, curriculum and instructional materials draw extensively from USA or European sources. For instance, Cumming's 1990 survey identified 234 teacher reference books or curriculum materials produced since 1975 by Canadians regarding ESL education, and only a handful prior to that date. Of these publications, most originated from just a few institutions in just a few cities. Extensive teacher education programs for adult ESL have developed in the past two decades at many Canadian universities and colleges, though most such programs still remain structurally separate from general programs of teacher education or in-service development (Mollica and Yalden 1984). These teacher-preparation and other professional orientation programs are in considerable demand, particularly in major cities, where a growing number of Canadians become professionally involved with ESL education each year. But funding for research and institution building in this area remains scarce, directed at short-term goals, and hardly sufficient to develop either comprehensive analyses and theories or analysts and theorists. To some extent, resources for English language education have remained limited—in comparison to other nations like the USA or Britain—because Canada has only rarely pursued an active policy of English as a Foreign Language education overseas (eg, with China in the 1980s; see Burnaby et al. 1986).

References

Acosta, J. (ed.) 1981-present *The West Coast Reader*. Langley, BC: BC Ministry of Advanced Education/Capilano College.

Allen, P. and Swain, M. 1984 Language in education: the Canadian context. *Language Issues and Education Policies*, ELT Documents 119. Oxford: Pergamon Press and British Council. 1–12.

Anderson, J. 1918 *The Education of the New Canadian: A Treatise on Canada's Greatest Educational Problem*. Toronto: J. M. Dent Sons.

Ashworth, M. 1988 *Blessed with Bilingual Brains: Education of Immigrant Children with English as a Second Language*. Vancouver: Pacific Educational Press.

Barman, J., Hebert, Y. and McCaskill, D. (eds) 1986 *Indian Education in Canada: Vol. 1. The Legacy*. Vancouver: UBC Press.

Barman, J., Hebert, Y. and McCaskill, D. (eds) 1987 *Indian Education in Canada: Vol. 2. The Challenge*. Vancouver: UBC Press.

Beiser, M. 1988 *After the Door Has Opened: Mental Health Issues Affecting Immigrants and Refugees in Canada*. Ottawa: Secretary of State, Multiculturalism; Health and Welfare Canada.

Boyd, M. 1992 Immigrant women: language, socio-economic inequalities, and policy issues. In B. Burnaby and A. Cumming (eds) *Socio-political Aspects of ESL in Canada*. Toronto: OISE Press. 141–59.

Burnaby, B. 1982 *Language in Education among Canada's Native Peoples*. Toronto: OISE Press.

Burnaby, B. (ed.) 1985 *Promoting Native Writing Systems in Canada*. Toronto: OISE Press.

Burnaby, B. 1987 Language for Native, ethnic, or recent immigrant groups: What's the difference? *TESL Canada Journal 4*. 9–27.

Burnaby, B. and Beaujot, K. 1986. *The Use of Aboriginal Languages in Canada: An Analysis of the 1981 Census Data*. Ottawa: Secretary of State of Canada.

Burnaby, B. and Cumming, A. (eds) 1992 *Socio-political Aspects of ESL in Canada*. Toronto: OISE Press.

Burnaby, B., Cumming, A. and Belfiore, M. 1986. *Formative Evaluation of the China–Canada Language and Cross-Cultural Program*. Toronto: OISE.

Burnaby, B., Harper, H. and Peirce, B. 1992. English in the workplace: an employer's concerns. In B. Burnaby and A. Cumming (eds) *Socio-political Aspects of ESL in Canada*. Toronto: OISE Press. 304–29.

Canada Employment and Immigration Advisory Council 1991 *Immigrants and Language Training*. Ottawa: Employment and Immigration Canada.

Canadian Bureau for International Education 1981 *The Right Mix: Report of the Commission on Foreign Student Policy*. Ottawa: CBIE.

Canadian School Trustees' Association 1989 *Scholastic Adaptation and Cost Effectiveness of Programs for Immigrant/Refugee Children in Canadian Schools*. Ottawa: Authors.

Churchill, S. 1986 *The Education of Linguistic and Cultural Minorities in the OECD Countries*. Clevedon, Avon: Multilingual Matters.

Coelho, E. 1988 *Caribbean Students in Canadian Schools*. Toronto: Carib-Can.

Corson, D. 1994 Minority social groups and non-standard discourse: towards a just language policy. *Canadian Modern Language Review 50*. 271–95.

Cumming, A. 1990 An annotated bibliography of Canadian ESL materials. Special issue 2 of *TESL Canada Journal*.

Cumming, A. 1991 *Identification of Current Needs and Issues Related to Adult ESL Instruction in British Columbia*. Richmond, BC: Open Learning Agency. [ERIC ED 353 855.]

Cumming, A. and Gill, J. 1991 Learning ESL literacy among Indo-Canadian women. *Language, Culture and Curriculum 4*. 181–200.

Cumming, A., Hart, D., Corson, D. and Cummins, J. 1993 *Provisions and Demands for ESL, ESD, and ALF Education in Ontario Schools*. Toronto: Modern Language Centre, Ontario Institute for Studies in Education. ONTERIS.

Cumming, A. and Mackay, R. 1993 *Evaluation of Phase 3 of SEVEC's Multicultural/Anti-racist Leadership Exchange Program*. Ottawa: Society for Educational Visits and Exchanges in Canada.

Cumming, P., Lee, E. and Oreopoulos, D. 1989 *Access: Task Force on Access to Professions and Trades in Ontario.* Toronto: Ontario Ministry of Citizenship.

Cummins, J. (ed.) 1984 *Heritage Languages in Canada: Research Perspectives.* Toronto: OISE.

Cummins, J. 1988 From multicultural to anti-racist education: an analysis of programmes and policies in Ontario. In T. Skutnabb-Kangas and J. Cummins (eds) *Minority Education: From Shame to Struggle.* Clevedon, Avon: Multilingual Matters. 127–57.

Cummins, J. 1989 Heritage language teaching and the ESL student: fact and friction. In J. Esling (ed.) *Multicultural Education and Policy: ESL in the 1990s.* Toronto: OISE Press. 3–17.

d'Anglejan, A. and De Koninck, Z. 1992 Educational policy for a culturally plural Québec: an update. In B. Burnaby and A. Cumming (eds) *Socio-political Aspects of ESL in Canada.* Toronto: OISE Press. 97–109.

Early, M. and Hooper, H. (eds) 1992 *ESL Students in Content Classes: A Task-based Resource Book.* Victoria: Queen's Printer.

Elson, N. 1992 The failure of tests: language tests and post-secondary admissions of ESL students. In B. Burnaby and A. Cumming (eds) *Socio-political Aspects of ESL in Canada.* Toronto: OISE Press. 110–21.

Faries, E. 1989 Language education for native children in northern Ontario. In J. Esling (ed.) *Multicultural Education and Policy: ESL in the 1990s.* Toronto: OISE Press. 144–53.

Haig-Brown, C. 1988 *Resistance and Renewal: Surviving the Indian Residential School.* Vancouver: Tillacum Press.

Immigration Canada 1991 *Annual Report to Parliament, Immigration Plan for 1991–1995, Year Two.* Ottawa: Employment and Immigration Canada.

Jones, S. 1992 Literacy in a second language: results from a Canadian survey of everyday life. In B. Burnaby and A. Cumming (eds) *Socio-political Aspects of ESL in Canada.* Toronto: OISE Press. 203–20.

Lewis, S. 1992 *Report on Race Relations in Ontario.* Toronto: Publications Ontario.

McAndrew, M. 1993 *The Integration of Ethnic Minority Students Fifteen Years after Bill 101: Some Issues Confronting Montreal's French Language Public Schools.* Ms. Montreal: Universite de Montreal, Centre d'Etudes Ethniques.

Mackay, R. and Myles, L. 1989 *Native Student Dropouts in Ontario Schools.* Toronto: Ontario Ministry of Education.

Mallea, J. 1989 *Schooling in a Plural Canada.* Clevedon, Avon: Multilingual Matters.

Ministere de l'Education, Gouvernement du Québec. 1981, 1983, 1984, 1986 *Programmes des etudes, Anglais langue seconde.* Québec: Authors.

Mohan, B. 1986 *Language and Content.* Reading, MA: Addison-Wesley.

Mollica, A. and Yalden, J. 1984 *English and French as Second Languages in Teacher Education Institutions.* Welland, Ontario: Canadian Modern Language Review.

Mougeon, R. and Heller, M. 1986 The social and historical context of minority French language education in Ontario. *Journal of Multilingual and Multicultural Development 7*. 199–227.

Ontario Ministry of Education 1988 *Curriculum Guideline. English as a Second Language and English Skills Development: Intermediate and Senior Divisions.* Toronto: Queen's Printer.

Ontario Ministry of Education and Training 1993 *Antiracism and Ethnocultural Equity in School Boards: Guidelines for Policy Development and Implementation.* Toronto: Queen's Printer.

Painchaud, G. 1993 L'enseignement des langues aux jeunes Québecois des communautes culturelles: Politiques et programmes. *Journal of the Canadian Association of Applied Linguistics 15*. 7–22.

Pendakur, R. 1990 *Speaking in Tongues: Heritage Language Maintenance and Transfer in Canada.* Ottawa: Secretary of State, Multiculturalism and Citizenship Sector.

Pendakur, R. 1992 Labor market segmentation theories and the place of immigrants speaking neither English nor French in Canada. In B. Burnaby and A. Cumming (eds) *Socio-political Aspects of ESL in Canada.* Toronto: OISE Press. 160–81.

Pendakur, R. and Ledoux, M. 1991 *Immigrants Unable to Speak English or French: A Graphic Overview.* Ottawa: Secretary of State of Canada, Policy and Research, Multiculturalism Sector.

Rodriguez, C. and Sawyer, D. 1990 *Native Literacy Research Report.* Salmon Arm, BC: Native Adult Education Resource Centre, Okanagan College.

Ryan, J. 1989 Disciplining the Innut: normalization, characterization, and schooling. *Curriculum Inquiry 19*. 379–403.

St Lawrence, I. 1989 *Aging Together: An Exploration of Attitudes towards Aging in Multicultural Ontario.* Toronto: Ontario Advisory Council on Senior Citizens.

Thomas, D. 1990 *Immigrant Integration and the Canadian Identity.* Ottawa: Employment and Immigration Canada.

CHAPTER 6

ENGLISH AND PLURALISTIC POLICIES: THE CASE OF AUSTRALIA

Joseph Lo Bianco
Chief Executive, Language Australia

Introduction

The secure place of English has been a central explanatory factor in the evolution of multilingual policies in Australia. Although English has no *de jure* status as national or official language it does occupy all major domains of public life. With such *de facto* dominance, the unassailed position English commands has greatly contributed to reversing the historical pattern of restrictive languages planning in education, and in other areas of public life and culture, that has been typical until recent decades.

However, some recent signals of a more restrictive orientation may be taking root in government attitudes at both the federal level and in some state administrations.

Overview of language planning in Australia

With the occasional exception where public authorities intruded into the realm of private and community decisions about language, the general pattern of policy-making has been an implicit or covert one. The desired outcome, whether through deliberate intervention or tolerant neglect has, until recent decades, been a simple and unambiguous goal: universal English monolingualism modelled on southern British norms, with elite foreign language teaching designed primarily as a form of tertiary access selection.

The primary means for attaining this goal have been the following:

- Outright hostility shown to the speakers of Australia's more than 270 indigenous languages. The dramatic cultural and personal dislocation, including forcible family break-up, whilst not directly aimed at language genocide, had this effect for a large number of the languages that can be termed Australian languages

- Stigmatisation and deprecation of Australian varieties of English

- Neglect and denigration of immigrant languages other than English

- General neglect of second language teaching and of Australian Sign Language.

The almost complete reversal of these negative goals over a long period, culminating in explicit national policies on language issues, has come after an even longer period of belief in a homogeneous cultural pattern for the nation with its associated linguistic counterpart: monolingualism.

From Clyne's (1991) analysis of the policies of this period it is clear that during the nineteenth century generally tolerant attitudes toward languages other than English had been common in all the British colonies that in 1901 federated to form the Commonwealth of Australia. With the exception of Aboriginal languages, public authorities did not actively, and often not even implicitly, discourage the use and promotion of languages other than English. It was only with the commencement of institutionalised formal education in the 1870s that English came to be allocated a competitive and key role. Chinese, French, German, Irish and Scots Gaelic, and Italian had been widely spoken and taught in many areas. Even with the federation of the colonies in 1901, generally accepting policies prevailed.

Nevertheless, restrictive immigration policies and war hostilities caused public authorities to intervene directly to modify the language behaviour of the population. Anti-Asian immigration laws and vicarious hostility to the Kaiser's Germany were the keys that opened the door of explicit and negative language policy. Legislation forcibly converting German-medium schools to English-only schools, or closing such schools altogether, was passed in several states. Extensive renaming of buildings, towns, and districts was imposed. Significant organised oppression of Aboriginal languages was also a characteristic of this period.

Although in a far less intense way than this, the period from the end of the First World War to the end of the Second World War saw generally monolingualist policies prevail. Despite its openly ethnocentric purposes, much of the immigrant recruitment program of the vast Post-War Migration Scheme led directly to an intensification of the diversity of the Australian population. This demographic pluralism, which in birthplace and linguistic origin terms is the second highest in the world after Israel's, laid the basis for the ultimate reversal of negative language policies (CAAIP 1986).

In recent decades progressively more positive orientations towards multilingualism have been a feature of public policy—both in educational and non-educational spheres. It is my view that to a significant degree these have been made possible by the perceived security of the status of English.

Language policies since the 1960s

From the middle of the 1960s there has been an almost uninterrupted evolution of progressively more explicit statements on language issues concerning minorities as well as progressively more positive valuations about these issues. Language policies have, however, usually been a subset of a broader culturally pluralistic orientation in the settlement of newly arrived immigrants. During the late 1970s explicit or deliberate attempts to highlight language issues as such emerged. As policies themselves have become more public and more accountable so too have they declared more fully a national interest in the cultivation of the linguistic resources of the population for the economic, cultural, and educational benefit. These have oscillated between two opposite poles of emphasis, occasionally emphasising the rights and opportunities for, and of, minority groups, at other times emphasising broader national benefit deriving from pluralism. The former is based on overcoming ethnically based inequalities, in particular the unequal segmentation of the labour market; the latter seeks some neutralising of the political effects of a rights-equality approach.

Despite a significant measure of expedient politicians' rhetorical affirmation of diversity ("rich mosaics of culture interacting") and despite a strongly contesting school of thought that holds that pluralist notions of society are invariably used by dominant groups to entrench inequalities or to confound the true economic bases of inequality— despite these, the majority of the development of policy since the late 1960s has been genuinely progressive and pluralistic.

The following have been key steps in laying the foundations for overall policies today:

1. The success of the 1967 referendum transferring responsibility for Aboriginal affairs from the state and territory governments to the Commonwealth, or federal, government

2. The passing of the 1971 *Immigration (Education) Act*, in which the Commonwealth explicitly recognised its primary responsibility for the settlement and language education of newly arrived immigrants

3. The concessions granted in two states (Victoria and South Australia) in the mid-1970s for bilingual, community language maintenance and multicultural programs

4. The initiation by the federal authorities of Aboriginal bilingual programs in the early 1970s in areas of Commonwealth jurisdiction

5. The accession by Britain to the European Community, which forced Australian exporting industries to reassess their traditional markets and to conclude that the future lay in the potential (now booming) markets of Asia, this economic stimulus leading to a wider self-definition for Australia

6. The neglect and decline of second language teaching, which mobilised language professionals to give legitimacy to the demands by ethnic and Aboriginal groups for a national language policy

7. The coalition of interests between ethnic, Aboriginal, and other groups creating a coherent and unified constituency for languages which was able to generate a sophisticated set of demands on government "when the time was right" (Lo Bianco 1988).

These seven developments have led to more open multilingual policies of today.

The culmination of these developments was the adoption of, and in 1987 the full funding of, Australia's first *National Policy on Languages* (Lo Bianco 1987) and its use as a model by most states for complementary policies. (The preceding two years had seen a Senate inquiry conclude that such a policy would be desirable.) Despite its revision (DEET 1991) via the 1991 *Australian Language and Literacy Policy* de-emphasising its pluralistic character and despite the present stress on English literacy, there is substantial funding and broad public acceptance of pluralism in languages policy in Australia today. This extends beyond school or educational settings to the use of now widespread interpreting and translating facilities for the community, multilingual public and private broadcasting, and research via the National Languages and Literacy Institute of Australia.

The most recent policy statement was the adoption by the Council of Australian Governments of the report *Asian Languages and Australia's Economic Future* in February 1994. This policy sets out an ambitious aim of having a majority of all students studying one of four languages (Chinese, Japanese, Indonesian or Korean) by the year 2006.

Debates and issues on language policy today

Language debates are still highly contested and vigorous today. The nativist English-only position seems now to have gone dormant. Arguments for languages policy-making fluctuate between two ends of a continuum of discussion. One set of arguments derives from the multicultural ethos and argues for schooling to develop children's potential bilingualism into an intellectual and cultural resource. The other derives from the imperatives of economy and the perceived need for Australia to drastically, and quickly, increase its Asian language skills. Pluralism and regionalism, however, are reconciled with the general projections of our population if present immigration trends from Asia are sustained.

Essentially, the multicultural argument is for status planning on behalf of minority languages. The economic argument is for acquisition planning (Cooper 1989) on behalf of languages perceived to be of significance in economic and geo-political terms. It would be wrong to give the impression that there are not significant tensions and disputes in language policy-making and in the priorities of the different advocacy groups.

The demands for Australia's full integration into the Asian region are not contested politically. Both major ideological groupings in the political spectrum in Australia advocate the full integration into the economically dynamic region of Southeast and North Asia. The world in general appears to be galvanising into gigantic trading blocks: Europe, the North American free trade zone, and the Asian-Pacific area. Despite the emergence of revived nationalist tendencies in some parts of the world the developed nations are so interdependent economically that *Homo economicus* speaks with a more persuasive voice than the proponents of national cultural protectionism. Australia's long history of "Asia-avoidance" is giving way to an enthusiastic, if (at times) self-interested, embrace. Language choices governed by geography and economics follow on inexorably.

But such changes cannot just be willed; new domestic competence and consciousness discards sentimental old attachments in favour of pragmatic choices and are able to bring them about. For some years, for example, Japanese has been the most widely studied and taught language in our higher education system and more Indonesian is taught in Australia than anywhere else except Indonesia. Asian cultural studies are now widely expected in social education curricula and syllabuses. Unlike the situation in the United States where a single language group (despite its diverse national origins) predominates as a sort of "majority-minority", nor the Canadian or Belgian situations with territorially-based minorities, Australia's diversity is distributed throughout its territory and is not dominated by any single language group. In this way the domestic challenges of pluralism are unlike those in North America. The ambitious policies on language can be premised on the common adoption of English. I believe these two points are crucial differences between the Australian case and the Canadian/American ones.

The reality of language study, however, as against the policy positions, which are generally positive, is far from satisfactory.

During the 1980s the Australian Bureau of Statistics conducted a sample survey of 100 000 adults, asking them to describe their language knowledge and use patterns. Of the approximately 8 million adults extrapolated from the sample, the vast majority of bilinguals were among the almost two million non-English language background adults who had added English to their first language.

The English-speaking-background Australians were, on average, far less well represented among those classed as bilingual. When the various census results were added (Clyne 1992), it was clear that in macro terms Australia's bilingual competence was by and large an immigrant and an Aboriginal phenomenon. Among the English speakers who claimed to be bilinguals were the enthusiasts, the language teachers, the privileged, and the well travelled. The majority of adults were steadfastly monolingual English speakers. The picture for children was more complex, but in broad terms it was clear that bilingual attainment was exceptional for English-language-background children; and for many bilingual children theirs was a transient achievement, a transitional bilingualism, which the Canadians have called subtractive as against additive bilingualism.

The much more assertive policies of more recent years may turn this around. Enrolments in LOTE (languages other than English) are on the increase and the newly found instrumental motivations could well bring about more positive language outcomes in future studies.

The report of the Council of Australian Governments, the annual meeting of state Premiers with the federal government, adopted its 1994 resolution declaring the national urgency of drastically upgrading languages teaching, especially of Chinese, Japanese, Indonesian and Korean (ie, justifying language study on economic grounds). It has become a commonplace to cajole and exhort Australians to pursue relations with Asia. These sentiments are represented in the 1988 Australia Day statement by the then federal Minister for Education that "our future is in Asia. We will either succeed in Asia or perish in it. We cannot change the reality of our geographical position and therefore must face up to that reality and develop a positive strategy to ensure our survival and our future prosperity" (Dawkins 1988).

An analysis of recent political discourse would reveal a dramatic reconstruction of the prevailing ideas of national culture and the significance of Australia's geographic location. It contains an urgent sense of a nationally reconstructive purpose. Multiculturalism, largely built on European origins, will need to find a reconciliation or an intersection of interest with such economically driven regionalism. The tension between these two discourses—multiculturalism and economically driven pressure for Asian integration—is the major issue in Australian language policy today. Immigration patterns, as previously stated, may assist in this process of reconciliation. The discursive emblem of the link between domestic multiculturalism and globalisation-regionalism is a new term: productive diversity. This rhetorical device has emerged from the Prime Minister's Office of Multicultural Affairs and appears to be gaining currency as the bridging concept between the local context and the global environment so that multicultural policy can be construed as a positive contribution to Asian integration. It remains to be seen if the policy of productive diversity can achieve this goal.

English

Australian English

Recent years have also witnessed a tardy and still incomplete but strong consciousness about the national character of English in Australia. As late as 1981, studies (see Gallois and Callan in Clyne 1989) found that Australians evaluated speakers of British English more favourably than speakers of Australian English, according to semantic differential analysis.

A significant breakthrough in acknowledging Australian English has been the publication of the *Macquarie Dictionary*. Despite some persisting problems of acceptance in the schools, the *Macquarie Dictionary* represents "an outstanding piece of language planning of a national variety of a pluricentric language" according to Clyne (1989:36). It is a dictionary of English from an Australian standpoint, giving Australian pronunciation, and listing Australian definitions ahead of English or American definitions where meanings differ.

Standard Australian English has also been expressly declared by the *National Policy on Languages* (as accepted in the Commonwealth Parliament in 1987) as the "shared, convenient and national language of Australia". This explicit endorsement also accepted the varieties, both social and geographic, of the language. The *Australian Language and Literacy Policy* declared that "Australian English is integral to Australian identity. It is the vehicle for mainstream Australian culture" (DEET 1991).

Despite such seemingly unproblematic progress it is probably not the case that ordinary Australians unambiguously accept these declarations. In addition there is strong academic contestation of the assertions about the Australianness of Australian English. In his highly critical piece on the elevation of Australian English to official status in Australian language policy, Doecke (1993) argues that we should be sceptical of contriving nationalism via language. He locates such an activity with celebrating kookaburras and blue gums as a sort of ideological manipulation to disguise important issues of national crisis in the economy and in social life. Doecke's reaction is to the way in which the national character of English was celebrated in the same document whose primary purpose was the promotion of English literacy for assisting processes of micro-economic reform (Moore 1996). The more pragmatic and popular acceptance of Australian models of English is almost universally accepted.

Turner (1991:35), in his analysis of trends in research into Australian English, comments that the accepted view with studies of Australian English is that we are dealing with "English in Australia rather than the studies of an Australian language". He states, "There is an increasing awareness that Australian English is not a single invariant entity. Besides varieties based on contact with Aboriginal languages, there are pockets of influence from the home languages of various immigrants" (p. 43). Whilst there may be low levels of lexical transfers into English as it is used in Australia (Ramson 1966:154–60), studies of communication, phonology, and pragmatics are showing an interesting and significant impact of multilingualism on English use in Australia.

Horvath (1991:305), for example, argues that migrants have had an impact in changing the character and pattern of the overall speech community, commenting that to exclude them from these fields of study or to treat their English as transitional towards the mainstream pattern "may well overlook important sources of change within the speech community". Studying the vowel patterns of first- and second-generation Italians and Greeks in Sydney, she shows that, although the marked linguistic pattern of the first generation can be tracked onto the widely accepted range of Broad, General, and Cultivated English (identified by Mitchell and Delbridge in 1965), an Ethnic Broad category can be identified; and that there is a lesser tendency among Greeks at least (and, though less strongly, among Italians) to emphasise the General as a way to diverge from the British Cultivated end of the continuum. She speculates that this is because these speakers have "never called England home" and their need to mask their distance from it is less felt. Such a pattern, if it were strong enough, could alter the ratio of users of the different varieties altogether.

The propagated norms of English in broadcasting and in education now derive almost exclusively from Australian sources, though North American influences are also evident. This replaces the modelling of Australian speech on British Received Pronunciation encouraged in schools and enforced on the Australian Broadcasting Commission until the Second World War.

Aboriginal English

Ambivalence towards standard and non-standard forms of Australian English can be acute in relation to Aboriginal English. The findings of the Enquiry into Aboriginal and Torres Strait Islander Languages Maintenance by the House of Representatives in 1992 concluded:

> There are a range of dialects of English known collectively as Aboriginal English. Aboriginal English is regarded by linguistics as a valid, rule-governed language capable of expressing the wide range of human experience. The failure to recognise it as a separate dialect leads to several problems. Many teachers still treat Aboriginal English as an uneducated or corrupted form of standard Australian English. Children learn best when the school makes use of their language development prior to school.

> While Aboriginal English and standard Australian English are mutually intelligible there are major differences in vocabulary, grammar, meaning, sounding system, gesturing and sociocultural context. The committee believes that the failure by schools and teachers to identify, accept and take into account the separate features of Aboriginal English is a major factor in Aboriginal children's poor performance in school. In courts and hospitals, the failure to identify and comprehend Aboriginal English significantly limits the effectiveness of those institutions (House of Representatives 1992:2).

Although curriculum writers and teacher trainers attempt to inculcate accepting attitudes and sociolinguistically sophisticated understandings of Aboriginal varieties of English it is unlikely to be the case that educational practice is affected by such moves.

Conclusion

Romaine (1991) comments that Australia is the first of the major Anglophone countries to formulate an explicit language policy. In its 1994 report the committee set up by the Council of Australian Governments to plan the 2001 centenary of political federation celebrated pluralistic language policies as a great achievement of Australian democracy.

In Australia, language planning and language-in-education planning have become remarkably well accepted. "English-speaking" countries have been reluctant converts to national language planning. In the past in Australia, language planning had been regarded in one or other of several, usually negative, ways:

First, as an activity of nation-building in post-colonial situations in which the imperatives of nationalism impelled certain countries to cultivate and carve out a role for an indigenous language to supplant the coloniser's tongue;

Second, as a response from Australian public authorities who regarded language policies as an activity of non-English-speaking countries wishing to gain access to technical literature and specialised knowledge, usually in English; and

Third, as the continental European nationalist predilection for cultivating (and quarantining from borrowings) a language seen as culturally prestigious.

As I have tried to show, language policy is now an accepted part of public discourse in Australia. It attempts to reconcile the sometimes divergent tendencies of domestic pluralism and economically motivated regionalism. I have also argued that the unchallenged primacy of English as the "shared, convenient and national language", especially with its newfound national distinctiveness, has been the solid ground on which diversity has been made possible. But the disputes about the "latitude" to allow minority language speakers, the public cost of services for multilingualism, and the effectiveness of the sometimes grandiloquent plans for language teaching are recurring themes in debate on language policy and more widely. The challenge for those educators who teach and research English for speakers of other languages is to regard group and individual bilingualism as their goal too. Children and adults who learn English as a second language do not have a mental *tabula rasa* on which English is inscribed. Their inevitable bilingualism can either be transitional and problematic or it can be assisted to become a stable, intellectually enriching, and socially esteemed accomplishment.

References

CAAIP (Secretariat to the Committee to Advise on Australian Immigration Policies) 1987 Understanding Immigration. Canberra: Australian Government Publishing Service.

Centenary of Federation Advisory Committee 1994 *2001: A Report from Australia.* Canberra: Australian Government Publishing Service.

Clyne, M. G. 1991 Australia's language policies: Are we going backwards? *Current Affairs Bulletin 68.6.* 13–20.

Clyne, M. G. 1992 *Community Languages in Australia.* Oxford: Oxford University Press.

Cooper, R. 1989 *Language Planning and Social Change.* Oxford: Oxford University Press.

Coulmas, F. (ed.) 1981 *A Festschrift for the Native Speaker.* The Hague: Mouton.

Coulmas, F. (ed.) 1994 Why is language standardization necessary? *Economic Considerations.* Tokyo: NLRI.

Dawkins, J. S. 1988 Challenges and opportunities: our future in Asia. In E. M. McKay (ed.) *Challenges and Opportunities: Our Future in Asia.* Asian Studies Association of Australia. Melbourne: Morphett Press. 13–21.

Department of Employment, Education and Training 1991 *Australia's Language: The Australian Language and Literacy Policy .* Vols 1 and 2. Canberra: Australian Government Publishing Service.

Doecke, B. March 1993 Kookaburras, blue gums, and ideological state apparatuses. *English in Australia.* 14–25.

Edwards, J. 1985 *Language, Society and Identity.* London: Basil Blackwell.

Gallois, J. and Callan, M. 1981 Cited in M. G. Clyne 1989 The Macquarie dictionary. In T. McNamara and C. Candlin (eds) *Language, Culture and Communication.* Sydney: NCELTR, Macquarie University Press.

Horvath, B. M. 1991 Finding a place in Sydney: migrants and language change. In S. Romaine (ed.) *Language in Australia.* Cambridge: Cambridge University Press. 304–18.

House of Representatives Enquiry into the Maintenance of Aboriginal and Torres Strait Islander Languages 1992 *A Matter of Survival: Language and Culture.* Canberra: Australian Government Publishing Service.

Lo Bianco, J. 1987 *National Policy on Languages.* Canberra: Australian Government Publishing Service.

Lo Bianco. J. 1990 Making language policy: Australia's experience. In R. B. Baldauf, Jr., and A. Luke (eds) *Language, Language Planning, and Language Education in Australasia and the South Pacific.* Clevedon, Avon: Multilingual Matters.

Mitchell, A. G. and Delbridge, A. 1965 *The Speech of Australian Adolescents.* Sydney: Angus and Robertson.

Moore, H. M. In press Language policies as virtual realities: two Australian examples. *TESOL Quarterly* (Special Issue on Language Planning and Policy and the English Language Profession).

Moore, M. 1991 *Enchantments and Dis-enchantments in Language Policy.* Melbourne: Melbourne Studies in Education, University of Melbourne.

Ramson, W. S. *Australian English: An Historical Study of the Vocabulary 1788–1898.* Canberra: ANU Press.

Romaine, S. 1991 (ed.) *Language in Australia.* Cambridge: Cambridge University Press.

Turner, G. 1991 Australian English and general studies of English. In M. Clyne (ed.) *Linguistics in Australia: Trends in Research.* Academy of the Social Sciences. 35–55.

CHAPTER 7

WHY ARE WE WAITING?
LANGUAGES POLICY DEVELOPMENT
IN NEW ZEALAND

Roger Peddie[13]
The University of Auckland, New Zealand

Introduction

In May 1987, after some years of planning and deliberation, Australia adopted its first *National Policy on Languages* (Lo Bianco 1987). An updated policy followed in 1991 (*Australia's Language: The Australian Language and Literacy Policy 1991*). At about the same time, in neighbouring New Zealand, there were extended discussions, huge and unpaid efforts by a few key people, and finally a concerted approach to government. As a result, the Labour Minister of Education, Mr Philip Goff, announced that New Zealand too would develop a national languages policy. This decision was made in August 1990. By the end of 1991 a report on languages policy was completed (Waite 1992) and presented to the new National Government Minister of Education, Dr Lockwood Smith. Responses were received until October 1992, and these were analysed and forwarded to the Minister. The years passed, another election took place, but no announcement of a policy was made. This essay gives a brief overview of the current New Zealand context (early 1995) and examines some of the factors that may explain why we in New Zealand are still waiting.

[13] I would like to thank Marilyn Lewis and a number of other people who commented on earlier versions of this paper. I also acknowledge the assistance of the New Zealand Ministry of Education, the National Languages and Literacy Institute of Australia, and the University of Auckland, all of whom provided funding and support for the research from which this paper was developed.

The initial context: New Zealand

In New Zealand, English is the major language of government, trade, the media and social communication, but other languages are beginning to be spoken and used more widely. Unlike the situation in Australia, some quite critical language data are unavailable in New Zealand. The New Zealand census of recent years has not given any information on languages spoken, or known, or even full information on ethnic affiliation. There are figures showing the numbers of Maori, Pacific Island peoples, Indians, Chinese, and other groups, but European groups have usually been distinguished only by place of birth rather than by ethnic or cultural affiliation.

Thus it is impossible to know how many "Yugoslavs" there are in New Zealand, with estimates varying wildly from a few thousand to fifty or sixty thousand. This is because many people from former Yugoslavia have been in New Zealand since the nineteenth century. Furthermore, no information is available on which languages are spoken or retained by New Zealanders from that region, nor with which modern state they would identify; nor is there any detailed information on where in New Zealand they or their descendants live.

Much more serious, no up-to-date information is available on how many of the large indigenous Maori population are fluent in their own language. Estimates regularly appear even in reputable publications, but the last valid survey of *te reo Maori* "Maori language", is arguably Benton's important survey completed in the late 1970s (Benton 1979).

The 1991 population of New Zealand (3.37 million) comprised almost 80 per cent of European origin, most of whom are ethnically Anglo-Celtic[14]. The largest non-Anglo-Celtic *Pakeha* "European" group is almost certainly the Dutch, but with assimilation over the last 50 years in particular, a count of these people is almost impossible. As with Yugoslavic peoples, estimates vary wildly, but as many as fifty or sixty thousand might self-identify as Dutch.

About 12.9 per cent of the population are indigenous Maori. Pacific Islands peoples (of whom over half are Samoan) make up 4.7 per cent.

[14] These and other figures are drawn from various publications of the 1991 Census of Population and Dwellings, and from updates released by government agencies.

In both cases percentages of school-aged children are higher. Nearly 1.5 per cent are ethnic Chinese, and there are a number of smaller groups including Indians (some from Fiji) and Vietnamese. The fastest growing minority group in the past five years is the Chinese. This population doubled in the intercensus period 1986–91 and is now estimated to number over 50 000. Another smaller but rapidly growing group is the Korean community, which has grown to an estimated 8000, located mainly in New Zealand's largest city, Auckland. The relatively concentrated groupings of recent arrivals in Auckland and Wellington are not matched for earlier arriving groups. At the same time, urban drift and south-north drift have altered demographic patterns throughout the country. Much of this information is known informally, as a linguistic or ethnic map of New Zealand is not available. What is clear is that there are areas of high and low Maori and migrant density, both in terms of large regions and also within the major cities. Language policies in education need to take this fact into account.

While several other countries, and notably Australia, have developed comprehensive languages policies, the absence of policy in New Zealand has led to developments occurring in a piecemeal or informal way (Goff 1990:7; Peddie 1991a). This seems to be the case even where these developments have been quite dramatic, as with the expansion of *te kohanga reo* "Maori language preschools". The sections that follow give a brief overview of what has happened in key areas.

Te reo Maori

It is clear that *te reo Maori* "Maori language", has undergone a significant revival in New Zealand. The numbers of students in secondary schools studying *te reo Maori* rose from about 1500 in 1967 to 19 000 by 1987 and have continued to rise, although more slowly[15]. As mentioned earlier, there has been a huge rise in the number of children learning Maori outside the home with the advent of *te kohanga reo*. These total immersion preschools were begun in 1982, run by local community groups with some government support. There are now over 800 *kohanga reo* with about a quarter of the age group of Maori children attending. There are also about a dozen bilingual (state) primary schools and 28 *kura kaupapa*

---

[15] These and other figures come from *Education Statistics of New Zealand* (annual) or from data kindly supplied to the author by the Data Management and Analysis Unit, Ministry of Education, Wellington.

Maori—schools conducted on Maori lines with teaching in *te reo Maori*. Altogether, more than 250 primary and secondary schools offer at least some Maori-medium education to more than 14 000 students.

Numbers in university courses have risen, and there are informal indications that at least some Maori parents are learning or re-learning the language, partly in order to help their *kohanga*-based children retain it in later years and partly as a matter of personal pride and identity. *Te reo Maori* can be counted as a core value in Maori culture, and the language revival has been part of a wider cultural revitalisation that has been taking place since the late 1960s.

Nevertheless, it should not be thought that the revival is secure and all the major issues are resolved. In 1993, 22 657 secondary school students were learning Maori, a figure including more than 8000 non-Maori students. This represents approximately 10 per cent of all students. In the same year, there were just over 40 000 Maori students in secondary schools, so two-thirds were not learning their language. Only 281 (of 410) secondary schools were offering *te reo Maori* (some through correspondence), although this represents a sharp rise from the figures even of the early 1980s.

Te reo Maori is used regularly on the *marae* "Maori meeting place", and on almost all Maori social and ceremonial occasions—at meetings, weddings, funerals, and formal welcomes. It is used in some national radio broadcasts and television programmes—though generally still those of a specialised nature—and is now more regularly found in newspaper advertisements and announcements. It is only recently, however, that a number of newspapers would accept material in *te reo Maori*, and even now some still request the English translation be published as well. Radio has been the area of greatest movement, with a number of small independent stations now broadcasting in *te reo Maori* on a regular and extended basis.

The picture, then, is changing, although broader public opinion is still almost certainly sharply split. Callers on radio talkback programmes, for example, are just as likely to scorn any learning of *te reo Maori* as to advocate its widespread learning and use. Their main objection is its "uselessness" compared with "useful" languages like English. A significant minority of parents in one large secondary school curriculum survey (1991) listed Maori language and culture as something they definitely wanted less of in the school programme—and this in an area where Maori constituted a moderately high proportion of the population.

Teachers have mixed views. Two 1991 New Zealand surveys showed that about two-thirds of surveyed language teachers and secondary school principals were against compulsory Maori language in secondary schools, although some favoured compulsion in primary schools. Only 40 per cent of the principals and less than a third of the teachers favoured *te reo Maori*'s having official equal status with English in all areas of government.

Finally, recent discussions of New Zealand's language needs have almost exclusively focused on languages of trade and tourism. A close analysis of both the draft *National Curriculum of New Zealand* (1991) and the *New Zealand Curriculum Framework* (1993) suggests that *te reo Maori* is arguably seen by government as an important part of New Zealand's heritage rather than as a significant living language (Peddie 1991c).

Te reo Maori is one of New Zealand's national languages; it is spoken only in New Zealand. Maori are the *tangata whenua* "people of the land", the indigenous people. For these reasons, along with the more pragmatic observation that about 20 per cent of school-aged children are Maori, it is clear that *te reo Maori* should be a critical area of focus in a New Zealand national languages policy. Yet as this chapter was being written, a Maori delegation had recently returned from taking a case to the (British) Privy Council concerning a claim over government inaction and responsibility for the use of *te reo Maori*, with particular reference to state-owned enterprises in the media[16].

English and ESL

The role of English in New Zealand is at once clearcut and problematic. It is quite clear that English is the major language and that all citizens need fluency and literacy in English to participate fully in politics, society, and the economy. While it is true that some people appear to function reasonably well in these areas with very little spoken English, these

[16] The formal case was rejected, but the Privy Council still made it clear that they believed that the claimants had a number of legitimate areas of concern.

people need family or friends to act as interpreters in situations in which English is absolutely necessary. Also, an unknown number of adult English-speakers are functionally illiterate, and government assistance for programmes in this area is reportedly inadequate.

While the status of English may seem clear, it is curious to note that there is currently no legislation requiring English in the schools other than as a subject to be taught in the core curriculum (ie, up to Form V, or age 15). This allows the *kura kaupapa Maori* to teach quite legally all subjects in *te reo Maori*. Policy in this area may thus be regarded as "negative", in the sense that it appears to be assumed that students will gain competence in English both by living in an English-speaking community and by having schooling in English as the norm.

Not only is there no clear policy to reinforce the status of English, but the nature of the corpus may also be in need of clarification. New Zealand English is perhaps identifiable to linguists and teachers, but public recognition and acceptance of "New Zealand English" as a national language may need some refocusing of attitudes.

Compared to provisions in Australia, New Zealand programmes in ESL are somewhat piecemeal. Migrants may or may not receive adequate assistance on arrival, although there is a well-established reception programme for refugees in Auckland, as well as a small number of regionally based consultants to help schools. Two centres for intensive English-language study aimed at new arrivals are located in Auckland, and smaller programmes do exist elsewhere. Research in the late 1980s argued that large numbers of students were receiving no or inadequate assistance (Peddie and Penfold 1987).

A recent Ministry survey of non-English-speaking background (NESB) students (Atkinson 1992) showed that only about 5 per cent of the school population could be classed as coming from homes where English was not the main language used. Over half of these were Pacific Island peoples, half of whom in turn had been born in New Zealand. Just over 30 per cent of NESB students were classified as competent in English. This means that about 3.4 per cent of New Zealand primary and secondary students (just over 31 500) required ESL assistance. Just over 1300 were described as having no English skills at all.

A Ministry update based on figures for 1994 showed that this last number had risen to over 2700, with a similar rise in the total number needing assistance. These numbers are clearly manageable, but resources are still perceived as inadequate.

It would be difficult to describe in a few sentences the variety of community and private provisions for ESL. Some secondary schools offer night and/or day classes for adults. Community houses offer some programmes, as do some polytechnics and universities. A number of private language schools have emerged, particularly in Auckland, but their target is more likely to be overseas students and others seeking intensive short-term programmes. To sum up, for school-aged students there is still no certainty that they will receive the specialist help needed, while adults seeking assistance outside the main centres might well find facilities limited.

It may be concluded that there is an urgent need for policy and action concerning English and ESL in New Zealand. Significantly, there was comparatively little input from professional linguists to the ad hoc group working towards a national policy (see below), even though an active representative did participate. The (New Zealand) National Association for the Teaching of English has also played a comparatively minor role in deliberations to date (cf. Peddie 1992), despite strong interest from their professional leaders. This whole area is problematic; English is critically important, but its dominant role seems to have led to its being simply taken for granted by policy makers.

The first major shift, however, may have come at last with the *New Zealand Curriculum Framework* (1993). In both this document and the 1991 draft which preceded it, the rhetoric, at least, suggests that the importance of New Zealand English is being considered more formally and more clearly.

Languages other than English and Maori

Like many other countries which rely on overseas trade, New Zealand faces a potential dilemma in the field of languages other than English and Maori (LOTEM). The larger minority groups in the country, with the exception of the Chinese, speak languages with little direct trade significance. Secondly, the traditional languages taught in secondary schools and universities are widely thought to meet inadequately the same trade imperatives. However, that this is a somewhat false perception has been suggested elsewhere (cf. Peddie 1991b). Closer analysis of economic data shows that German and French, for example, are indeed among the top group of languages spoken in countries with whom New Zealand trades.

This observation, then, in no way negates the main point. Languages such as Standard Chinese (Mandarin) and Indonesian are not widely taught, Korean programmes are just emerging, and Arabic barely figures at all. Korean is taught in a few polytechnics and at the University of Auckland, where it is, in part, funded by Korean interests. Arabic is not taught in any school or university but is offered by some polytechnics.

The LOTEM currently taught in New Zealand vary across institutions. In the early childhood age groups, there are over 100 Pacific Island language immersion preschools, catering to almost 4000 children, and it is possible that a few other community groups are setting up similar schemes. Certainly, some ethnic community groups (Cantonese, Polish, and Hebrew, for example) have been holding after-hours language classes for many years, but mainly for school-aged children.

In primary schools, there is almost no LOTEM, although some of the two-year intermediate schools still have a little French or, less commonly, another introductory language programme. A major factor here is the relative lack of language qualifications among primary school teachers. With the recent move to BEd degree programmes in almost all primary teacher education courses, this situation may change, but the change will be slow unless language courses are promoted as being desirable for employment.

In secondary schools, a sharp increase in the teaching of Japanese has come about in part through parental and governmental pressure to introduce languages of trade. The situation for Japanese is, however, by no means ideal. In 1990, for example, over 400 students were studying Japanese by correspondence, and 47 schools were working through correspondence courses alone. Stories persist of some schools offering Japanese with underqualified teachers; a recent survey showed that approximately 10 per cent of those who responded had neither a degree nor were native Japanese speakers (Choi 1994).

French is still a widely taught language in secondary schools, although numbers are declining. In 1994 just under 11 per cent of all secondary school students were studying French, but more than half of these were in the third form, and many schools have only part-year courses at this level. About 11 per cent studied Japanese, 4 per cent studied German, while all other LOTEM combined totalled just under two per cent. These last-named LOTEM included Latin (1 per cent), Spanish, Russian, Indonesian, Samoan, Cook Islands Maori, and Standard Chinese. Based on recent figures, the enrolments in the final-year seventh form LOTEM courses are just over 10 per cent of the total student number. This figure would drop further if enrolments in more than one language are taken into account.

At the tertiary level, a similar range of languages is taught, with some interesting developments in some areas. This includes the combining of language courses with business and other studies at Waikato University. As noted earlier, Korean is now taught at Auckland University, while student numbers in Spanish and Italian are proportionately much higher in tertiary level courses than in secondary schools.

Offerings of language courses in polytechnics are becoming more extensive. They are also regarded by some as providing a greater depth in terms of communication skills, mainly because a "language" course at a university offers far more than just the language skills. Ascertaining the numbers of student enrolments in tertiary level courses is somewhat complex, however, as individual course/paper enrolments are needed as opposed to enrolments in subjects. Estimates based on figures from the late 1980s, and supported by recent informal data, suggest perhaps 5 per cent of students might be enrolled in a language course at university.

Finally, LOTEM are taught in adult and continuing education classes, notably by continuing education centres in the universities and in secondary school night classes. The number of such classes is quite large. Courses often begin full, but there are regular reports of high percentages of dropouts over the teaching year.

Overall, the picture for LOTEM is not as gloomy as some commentators imply. Nevertheless, three points may be made by way of conclusion. First, there is little coordinated planning as could be provided by a languages policy. Second, there are students studying to quite high levels in some languages of economic importance, but it is unclear whether they actually use their language skills in trade or tourism. Third, there are some serious questions to be asked about the qualifications and training of some of the teachers who are asked to teach LOTEM in New Zealand. Teaching certificates are not restricted by subject specialisation, so that a teacher working in a small school with only a first-year university language qualification and little or no training methods could be solely responsible for teaching that language. This is an area needing serious planning and urgent attention (*Languages for All* 1991).

Language services

"Language services" is the term used to cover a range of activities and structures which support and assist people whose languages are not those of the broader community. In New Zealand, this essentially means all those who are not fluent in English. I will consider three areas here: translation and interpreter services, electronic and print media, and libraries.

Translation and interpreting in New Zealand are carried out by a variety of state and private agencies. The New Zealand Society of Translators and Interpreters has pushed since its inception for high standards and for some form of regulation. There is a government translation service based in Wellington and a number of private agencies, mainly in Auckland and Wellington. No New Zealand-wide qualification exists, although Auckland University offers a Diploma in Translation. The use of examinations organised by the Australian organisation the National Accreditation Authority for Translators and Interpreters (NAATI) is becoming more common, and New Zealand links with this organisation are good. As in Australia, a level three qualification (of five) is regarded as the minimum desirable level for professionals.

The provision of qualified interpreters of New Zealand Sign Language is reportedly insufficient. This is an important interpreting area that can easily be overlooked. A number of business firms also reportedly have no idea of the skill levels required for competent translation; the universities are still rung up from time to time by firms requesting students to translate even such things as instructions for the use of chemicals. Some language teachers in smaller towns have had similar experiences, normally with no understanding (or acceptance) by the firm involved of the professional rates translators can justifiably charge.

Over the past five to ten years a positive move towards making materials on critical issues available in languages other than English has taken place. Most official government publicity material regularly provides Maori translations, and there is an increasing use of Samoan and other Pacific Islands languages. Hospitals, in particular, and other public institutions in Auckland and Wellington are also increasingly signposted in common LOTEM, and major hospitals are using native-speaking staff to interpret for NESB patients. While these moves are encouraging, a lack of widely available interpreting and translating services remains.

In related moves, shops and services in key tourist areas regularly have signs and some advertising material in Japanese, while land agents in Auckland are beginning to use Standard Chinese in some of their brochures. However small these developments may seem to the outsider, they are assisting to raise the profile of languages in the community. Yet the risk remains that some of the English-speaking majority will see such developments in a negative light. A recent well-publicised brawl involving Korean students at an Auckland secondary school signals the need for rapid moves on intercultural understanding.

The media present a similar piecemeal picture. There are, as noted earlier, radio stations in several areas broadcasting in *te reo Maori*, while community language stations in Auckland and Wellington have broadcast in other languages over the last few years. On television little is broadcast in *te reo Maori*, less in Pacific Islands languages, and almost nothing (the occasional subtitled foreign film apart) in other languages. Language-learning programmes have rarely been broadcast on the radio, and nothing is regularly available in any of the media for new learners of English. There are serious gaps in these areas.

Libraries can offer support to languages through materials for new learners of English and books and materials in common community and trade languages. With rare exceptions, outside of the main centres, such provisions appear to be minimal, especially in terms of materials for ESL.

Policy development

As made clear in the introduction, there is currently no clear comprehensive languages policy in New Zealand. English is the country's official language, while *te reo Maori* is officially recognised as a national language by the *Maori Language Act* of 1987. This Act established the Maori Language Commission, recognised the use of *te reo Maori* in parliament and the courts, and offered some official support for the language. Despite the beliefs of some New Zealand teachers and secondary school principals, this does not mean *te reo Maori* has equal status with English.

This fact was made clear in December 1991, when the Maori Language Commission objected to the minimal use of *te reo Maori* in New Zealand's new passports. In response to these criticisms, the Minister of Internal Affairs was reported to have said: "The official language status of Maori does not require Maori to be duplicated everywhere" (New Zealand *Herald,* 28 December 1991). The case noted above of Maori going to the Privy Council in November 1993 suggests that nothing major has changed. Nevertheless, *te reo Maori* is now regularly used in government brochures relating to, for example, parliamentary elections or social welfare benefits.

The need for languages policy has been recognised and promoted by several groups and individuals during the past 20 years. The New Zealand Association of Language Teachers (NZALT) has been interested in a comprehensive policy almost since its inception in 1974. In the early 1980s NZALT wrote to a number of ministries asking if they had a policy on languages; only one or two replied, in each case noting an ad hoc approach to language and language skills.

Similarly, in the mid-1980s, an officer in the Maori and Islands Division of the Ministry (NZ) reportedly proposed a quite comprehensive package of language support and development, based on principles that amounted to a languages policy in education. Only some relatively minor portions of the proposal were adopted. The same officer, Mr Christopher Hawley, worked tirelessly to promote the development of policies for languages in education in the late 1980s and was instrumental in the eventually major developments now to be described.

In 1988 the first national conference on ESL and community languages was held in Wellington. Following this conference, an ad hoc group was set up, based in Wellington, to develop proposals for a national languages policy. A draft document was prepared for a seminar held under teacher in-service provisions in Auckland in April 1989. A number of changes were made to the document during that week, and further minor changes were made after the new document was widely circulated later in the year. The document was finally released in a bilingual format in September 1989 under the title *Towards a National Languages Policy. Hei putake mo tetahi kaupapa reo mo Aotearoa.*

A delegation headed by Mr Walter Hirsh, former Race Relations Conciliator and longtime supporter of languages policy development, met with both the (Labour) Minister and the Associate Minister of Education late in 1989. After a request that the ad hoc group show more clearly how policy might impact other ministries was fulfilled, a delegation again met with the Minister of Education early in 1990. At both meetings the Minister, Mr Philip Goff, showed considerable interest and support.

In August 1990, a second ESL/community languages conference was held in Wellington. In a concluding address, the Associate Minister of Education, Mr Noel Scott, delivered a speech on behalf of the Minister in which the latter recognised the importance of language issues and acknowledged that these "issues associated with languages in New Zealand have been dealt with in an ad hoc way" (Goff 1990:7). The speech went on to announce that a national languages policy would be developed and that a person would be contracted during 1991 to carry out this development.

Financial support of the Ministry of Education for a longitudinal comparative study on languages policy (on which this chapter is based) began in 1988. Several other research contracts have considered aspects of language and language policy (eg, McPherson and Corson 1989). Nor has the Ministry been idle in attempting to develop policy strategies in a range of areas affecting language. These developments show that the Ministry has had an interest in languages policy for several years, but there is no public evidence of comprehensive planning.

Aoteareo (the Waite Report): Background

Several years of pressure by a variety of groups and ad hoc organisations came to an initially successful conclusion at the end of the second New Zealand Conference on ESL and Community Languages held in Wellington in August 1990. Following the change of government in the October 1990 elections and the appointment of Dr Lockwood Smith as Minister of Education, further representations by the ad hoc group helped to ensure that the earlier Labour government commitment was confirmed by the new ruling National Party. Dr Jeffrey Waite was appointed to develop a report that could lead to a national policy on languages for New Zealand. Waite, a former member of the Maori Language Commission, fluent in *te reo Maori* and holder of a Doctorate in applied linguistics, was well suited to the task. After conducting a large number of interviews and three national *hui* "meetings," of representative organisations, Waite presented his report to the government at the end of 1991.

Informants have reported that there were three versions of the Waite Report. The first, sometimes referred to as a working document, was circulated among a limited number of government organisations. This version contained a number of recommendations. After some rewriting, a second version had a limited release, notably to a committee chaired by Professor Robert Kaplan, a leading international researcher in languages policy and planning. After some further (minor?) rewriting, the report was released in two parts in early May 1992 under the title *Aoteareo: Speaking for Ourselves*. No recommendations in the document were released to the public.

The report appeared with a foreword by the Minister of Education and a call for submissions to be received by 1 October 1992. The submissions were independently analysed by a policy analyst in the Ministry, although earlier Ministry comment was that it would be analysed by an external firm of consultants. Following this analysis, a report was sent to the Minister late in 1992.

The analysis, released to the writer under the provisions of the *Official Information Act*, is an interesting mixture. Only 129 submissions were received, along with 94 duplicates from a TESOL organisation and 349 signatures on a petition regarding Latin. Only three submissions were received from Maori. The submissions and the subsequent analysis clearly show the limitations of an "open" response. As the Ministry analyst concludes:

> Owing to the unstructured nature of the submissions to this discussion paper, and the fact that responses could be taken into account only if issues were specifically addressed, in addition to the small size of the overall sample, many of the results do not appear to be statistically significant (NZLP Report: Analysis of Responses, p. 10).

It is unclear what moves have been made since this time. In a letter to the researcher dated 1 April 1993, the Minister stated, "The New Zealand Languages Policy project is currently on the work programme of the Minister of Education". The letter went on to say that "there is as yet no projected date for the announcement of new policy in this area" (letter from the Hon. Dr Lockwood Smith, Minister of Education, 1 April 1993). Information later released by Ministry officials shows that in May 1993 the New Zealand Languages Policy project was formally replaced by three discrete developments: ESOL education and support; Asia 2000; and extending provisions in second language learning.

Despite this shift, and hints of further change, the Waite report remains important. Although released as a "discussion document" (*Aoteareo* 1992: Minister's Foreword), it is likely to provide at least the foundation for any policy that may emerge in the near future. It is therefore worth noting its main areas of interest.

Aoteareo (the Waite Report): Summary

The Waite Report is divided into two parts: a brief Overview and a longer section expanding on the Issues (Waite 1992). In the Overview, Waite identifies six main priorities. He notes that all six have in fact high priority and that there is some interrelationship among the six areas (Waite 1992, Part A:18). The six priorities areas are as follows:

1. Revitalisation of the Maori language
2. Second-chance adult literacy
3. Children's ESL and first language maintenance
4. Adult ESL
5. National capabilities in international languages
6. Provision of services in languages other than English (pp. 18–22).

Waite justifies the development of policy and discusses the government's responsibilities in languages. He also provides a good deal of background information on the languages scene in New Zealand and on the priority areas listed above. In addition, he offers an interesting section on language, including an argument regarding the need for better knowledge about linguistics and language issues generally.

Waite's discussions on the importance of *te reo Maori*, the needs of the deaf, and community languages and ESL are all informative and interesting. He is less detailed on literacy needs, not surprisingly, because the research base here is much less clear. On research needs he is brief, with one page right at the end of Part B, but to the point. Yet given the extremely important needs in this area (Peddie 1991d), this brevity is to be regretted.

The area in which perhaps Waite received most public criticism related to international languages. By focusing almost exclusively on economic needs, the report underplays the significance of the study of literature and the learning and appreciation of classical languages. For some critics, this particular point confirmed their belief that this was a utilitarian report, one that ignored the cultural and literary dimensions of language. This criticism has some justification. Furthermore, a complete reading of the report suggests in fact a somewhat uneasy balance between economically desirable proposals and those which could be classed under a social justice heading.

To assess either the long-term import or even the short-term impact of the Waite Report is difficult at this stage. Certainly, the report appears to be a significant step towards the development of policy, but both informal evidence and content analysis of the final version hint at some changes from an original document that may have argued much more strongly for a comprehensive and substantive policy. The strong arguments that appeared in earlier documents do appear, but in somewhat muted form. If there were only minor changes from the original this would be somewhat surprising, given that Waite made a substantial contribution to earlier developments (eg, *Towards a National Languages Policy for New Zealand* 1989).

Recent curriculum documents

A final hint of government moves in languages policy might well be found in the recent review of the compulsory core curriculum for New

Zealand schools. The review has been in progress, in one form or another, since 1983. Earlier documents that show some interest in languages, particularly with regard to English and Maori, have been reviewed elsewhere by this writer, but they include statements that do not offer more than encouragement for "opportunities" (Peddie 1993). The most significant documents in this sequence are *The New Zealand Curriculum Framework* (1993) and a discussion document called *Education for the 21st Century* (1993).

The Framework was released in mid-1993, two years after a draft document set out the main lines to be followed. In brief, it will be required that students be offered seven "essential learning areas", eight "essential skills", and selected attitudes and values. Learning areas, though, may be offered in or across traditional subjects. However, the subjects of English, science, and mathematics are to be compulsory.

One of the essential learning areas is "language and languages". Because this is expected to be the foundation document for curriculum over the next years, it is worth quoting the relevant statements from this section of the framework.

> . . . all students will need to develop the ability and confidence to communicate competently in English, in both its spoken and written forms. Provision will be made for students whose first language is not English. Students will have the opportunity to become proficient in Maori.
> The nature of mother tongue programmes will be decided by schools in response to local community needs and initiatives.
> Students will be able to choose from a range of Pacific, Asian, and European languages, all of which are important to New Zealand's regional and international interests (*The New Zealand Curriculum Framework* 1993:10).

Regardless of the positive statements that precede each of the above, a good deal of vagueness remains about what will actually be provided, and considerable choice is still left to schools. Second, it is entirely unclear how Latin or other classical languages might fit into this framework. Third, there is no indication that the government might be developing any comprehensive policy in this area, nor even a hint as to exactly how students are going to be able to choose from the "range" of (presumably appropriate) languages mentioned in the final quotation above.

The discussion document, released shortly after the Framework, is somewhat more definite in its support for languages. The document proposes ten main aims for education, one of which is "High levels of achievement in essential learning areas and essential skills throughout the compulsory school years". In discussing this aim, the document notes six targets, one of which is specifically for LOTEM. This sets a series of percentages of students who, by the end of the second year of secondary school, will be able "to converse with and write to a native speaker of a language other than English or Maori about simple, every-day matters" (*Education for the 21st Century* 1993:27). The percentage is set to reach 50 per cent by the year 2000, but no hint is given as to how this will be achieved.

Most significantly, the commercial value of languages is the reason offered in the text preceding the target. After presenting some "context" statements, the document goes on to say:

> While all learning areas are important, one indicator of the school system's ability to provide the skills needed by New Zealand's economy is the number of students who study other languages. At present 36 per cent of students study a language other than English for a period of at least two years at secondary school. Growth is desirable in this area (p. 26).

Despite the fact that the final document (*Education for the 21st Century* 1994) contains much less about these issues, it does seem clear that languages are gaining a higher profile both in the eyes of government and in terms of the curriculum (cf. below). But it is equally clear that this is more in terms of economic strategy than of the much wider range of issues that need to be covered by a comprehensive policy. It is now timely to look at some of the factors that relate to the development of such a policy.

Why are we waiting?

This brief survey of the initial context in New Zealand suggests that the languages scene is indeed very complex. In some areas, major changes have occurred, leading to a much greater awareness of language as an issue. This applies particularly and for different reasons to *te reo Maori* and to languages of trade and tourism. In terms of other language needs, provisions are uncoordinated and/or relatively scarce, particularly outside the major urban areas, or even (some argue) outside of

Auckland and Wellington. Those interviewed in New Zealand during the longitudinal study consistently spoke of the need for policy, for coordination, and for greater support. The needs are widespread; a comprehensive policy that can provide coordination and can establish immediate goals and set medium and longer-term priorities appears to be overdue. What then are the factors preventing or postponing an announcement of languages policy in New Zealand?

The reasons for the current absence of a comprehensive New Zealand national languages policy can be examined under five headings:

1. The shifting demographic context
2. *Te reo Maori:* the *tangata whenua,* "people of the land"
3. Government and its agencies
4. Business and wider society
5. The economy.

1. The shifting demographic context
As noted earlier in this chapter, New Zealand is undergoing some quite rapid changes in demography. Like Australia, the recent influx of Asian and, in particular, Chinese migrants has been both visible and widely discussed in the media. Not all the publicity has been good. Several wealthy Chinese have been subjected to armed burglaries in their homes. An Indian shopkeeper was bludgeoned to death by three teenagers wielding softball bats. The relatively quiet South Island city of Nelson was the scene of several racist incidents involving migrants, while the brawl in Auckland between *Pakeha* and Korean students has already been noted. All of these incidents took place within a few months in late 1993 and early 1994.

The recent Asian migration follows substantial increases in Pacific Island peoples from the 1970s. This all means that, along with the substantial Maori group (see below), minorities in New Zealand are mainly non-European. It can be suggested that one reason for the absence of a comprehensive policy may be linked to racist concerns about the place of these non-European groups in society.

2. *Te reo Maori:* The *tangata whenua*
While some Maori have been involved in recent moves towards a national languages policy, earlier moves involved mainly non-Maori groups. There has been a strong drive by Maori to establish a bicultural society, one of whose features would clearly be a high level of bilingual-

ism. Until fairly recently, some other groups in society have perhaps felt their own language needs ran counter to such an approach. Certainly, the widespread development of Maori preschools has been paralleled by the development of a number of Pacific Island language preschools, now numbering well over 100. As well, there has been a general acceptance of Maori priorities in language among those seeking to promote a languages policy.

Nevertheless, the general agreement among English and non-English-speaking groups over the need for a languages policy has taken place only in the last few years. The dominant role played by Maori revitalisation has also not been translated into strong and concerted support for a comprehensive policy. At a time, then, when Maori needs and aspirations are continuing to grow in strength, these same developments may have been one factor in preventing a comprehensive policy from emerging. And again, some racist nervousness about the possibility of compulsory Maori language in schools may well have been involved at both the public and the political levels of New Zealand society.

3. Government and its agencies

It is clear that in New Zealand, as elsewhere, the government and its agencies have played the deciding role in languages policy development. In New Zealand, developments have been firmly centred in the Ministry of Education, an approach strongly advised against by international language planning expert Professor Robert Kaplan during his consultancy visit in 1992. Within the Ministry it has mainly fallen to the lot of quite junior staff to work in this area. While not suggesting any resistance on their part, at no stage has there been a strongly committed senior officer working to promote a languages policy. Waite, for example, was based in the Ministry but has since moved to a different position. A 1993 draft document on languages policy was unsigned but was apparently written by another officer who had not been directly involved in this area previously.

Similarly, neither the present nor the previous Ministers of Education appear to have had a firm commitment to developing a national policy, despite a strongly worded statement by Goff in 1990 and full acceptance of the need to continue policy development by Smith. Until very recently, statements about the need for languages have in fact been made mainly by other Ministers, notably by the then Minister of External Relations and Trade (and Deputy Prime Minister), Mr Don McKinnon.

Yet the interdepartmental committee that advised Waite during preparation of *Aoteareo*, while representing some 20 departments and organisations, did not contain many who could be described as senior decision-makers.

Educationists in general have offered little public support. While language teachers and language teacher organisations have been very strong advocates of policy development, they have tended to act somewhat in isolation. The New Zealand Association of Language Teachers and the New Zealand Association of the Teachers of English, for example, have never held a joint conference or meeting specifically on languages policy. The Ministry of Education, therefore, has never been subjected to a united voice from substantial numbers of its teachers or schools.

An important further point needs to be made here. The move towards self-governing schools has left the issue of compulsion in the curriculum in a somewhat dubious state. As noted earlier, the government has made it clear that English, mathematics, and science are to be compulsory. The language and languages "essential learning area" of *The New Zealand Curriculum Framework* (1993), however, can be organised by individual schools in a variety of ways. There is no compulsion hinted at for any language other than English.

4. Business and the wider society
The New Zealand economy depends to a very large extent on export markets (see below), and increasingly these markets are located in non-English-speaking countries. New Zealand manufacturers, however, do not appear to have the awareness of language and cultural aspects that could do much to foster such markets. Advertisements for export companies signalling the desirability of LOTEM are extremely rare, although there has been a recent rise in the number of institutions offering commercial translating services. In an early meeting of the national advisory group seeking to develop a framework of nationally recognised units in language, the two representatives from industry both claimed to have almost no knowledge of language issues and language learning.

On the other hand, calls for New Zealand business people to learn more languages of trade and tourism have increased (eg, Callister and Haines 1991; Crocombe et al. 1991). The climate of awareness, then, may well be changing. Until this is translated into clearly defined needs, and well-publicised employment opportunities, this changing climate may not aid the development (or implementation) of policy.

The language communities themselves have not been active at a public and visible level. Certainly, strong informal indications of cultural and linguistic revitalisation among a wide range of ethnic minorities are evident. Many groups do have after-hours classes, although there is no clear parallel to government-provided ethnic school funding as in Australia. There is no sign of a concerted approach on language and no hint that such groups used their voting power to promote language (or cultural) issues in the 1993 election.

5. The economy
Apart from, but clearly related to, the interests of business, the economy itself is a major factor in the development of a national languages policy in New Zealand. In the face of a serious recession, both major political parties have followed a similar line in recent years. This has included turning some departments into state-owned enterprises, selling some completely (like the Bank of New Zealand and New Zealand Rail), and reducing government spending wherever possible. At the same time, emphasis on education for the economy, for skill training and for qualifications that can benefit the country as a whole has increased.

This has some interesting implications for languages and language policies. First, it has meant an increase in "business migrants", people who have capital and a background in enterprises. These people are increasingly demanding that quality ESL programmes are available in schools—often schools that previously had a tiny minority of Pacific Island or other migrant groups. Interestingly enough, the government does not seem to accept that putting money into quality ESL programmes will not only increase the likelihood that the recipients will not end up receiving the dole, but will also tend to ensure that migrants are able to utilise to the full whatever skills they bring with them to New Zealand (Peddie 1991d).

A further and very significant factor is the rise in earnings from tourism, now New Zealand's biggest earner of foreign exchange. While large numbers of tourists continue to arrive from English-speaking countries, the sharpest rises are from non-English-speaking countries, with the Japanese as the second-largest group after the Australians (Waite 1992).

These economic factors lie behind the recent calls for international languages of trade and tourism. It is significant that classical languages received scant mention in *Aoteareo* and that community languages are hardly ever mentioned in public statements by government Ministers. In some ways, therefore, the heightened profile for particular languages may even work against the development of a balanced and equitable policy, with a broad focus on learning languages for community, international and cultural purposes.

Next, a languages policy requires government money, and in significant quantities. The Australian and other policies have quite adequately demonstrated that point. In a climate in which government is publicly bent on reducing its core spending, the prospect of a policy decision costing millions of dollars cannot be particularly palatable. Yet this should not prevent the development and promulgation of a symbolic policy, with resources to be phased in if and when they are available. This was a major proposal put forward to government by Kaplan in 1992 (personal communication), while the writer believes that a symbolic policy might be received badly and be more risky politically to government (Peddie 1991d).

Concluding discussion

It is still possible that by the time this chapter is published New Zealand will have a National Languages Policy. The preceding analysis should not be seen as leading to a definite conclusion that such a policy will not appear. Rather, the analysis has attempted to show why New Zealand does not have a comprehensive policy at this point in time (early 1995), despite the promising moves made in late 1990 and 1991.

As indicated previously, the situation at present is complex. The economy is beginning to show signs of recovery, but unemployment remains high and the newly elected government cannot afford to begin a new spending round that could result in higher taxes or higher inflation, or both. This mitigates against the introduction of a comprehensive policy. Yet the increasing public emphasis on trade and external relations with Asia is very likely to result in government looking for ways to correspondingly increase the numbers of students taking international languages of trade at all levels of the education system. Education for the 21st Century (1993) in part established a new emphasis, but it lacks the detail to give confidence—and it is still only a discussion paper.

A vital consideration not mentioned previously is teacher supply. Close analysis here reveals a significant lack of qualified language teachers in New Zealand, particularly in some of the key languages of trade (eg, Korean, Arabic, Standard Chinese). Training quality language teachers takes a long time, and there are special difficulties of distance if teachers seek to spend some time in a country where their LOTEM is spoken (Peddie 1991d). These points have apparently been confirmed and highlighted in recent Ministry analysis. Introduction of compulsory language learning, therefore, might at this stage be totally counterproductive.

The key issues remain much the same, however, as when the major proposals were brought forward by the ad hoc groups in 1989 (*Towards a National Languages Policy* 1989). These include the following:

1. Should *te reo Maori* be compulsory?
2. Should any language be compulsory?
3. What role should there be in education for community languages?
4. Should there be support for selected "priority" languages?
5. Should "trade languages" receive special government support?
6. How should provisions in ESL be developed and improved?

Most of these issues cut right across what may be labelled a purely pragmatic argument for more students learning international languages of trade. And these arguments are often couched in terms that display a surprising ignorance about language and culture. There are calls for more students to learn Japanese, for example, when the needs appear to be for a small number of highly skilled Japanese speakers. The 1993 secondary school total of 2500 sixth and seventh formers may well be more than adequate—if they proceed to develop high level and appropriate skills (Peddie 1991b).

It may be more productive for the government in the immediate future to model and to encourage both jobs and higher salaries for people with these appropriate language skills. This may achieve their economic and pragmatic goals in the areas of language, while eliminating the necessity to create a comprehensive policy. It is difficult to see, though, how they can avoid a substantial upgrading of provisions in ESL and some further moves in *te reo Maori*. Whether a bundle of these initiatives will be put together and sold to the general public as a "languages policy" remains to be seen.

Whatever the outcome(s), New Zealand has considerable needs and considerable potential as well as facing considerable challenges in the area of language. A comprehensive national languages policy is highly desirable on cultural, economic, social, and equity grounds. Nevertheless, given the economic realities of our time, waiting for such a policy may well continue for some time yet.

References

Atkinson, A. 1992 *Non-English-speaking Background Students in New Zealand Schools*. Wellington: Ministry of Education.

Benton, R. A. 1979 *Who Speaks Maori in New Zealand?* Wellington: New Zealand Council for Educational Research.

Callister, P. and Haines, L. 1991 *Tomorrow's Skills*. Rev. ed. Wellington: New Zealand Planning Council.

Choi, D-K. 1994 *Japanese Language in New Zealand Secondary Schools*. Unpublished MEd thesis, University of Auckland.

Crocombe, G. T., Enright, M. J., Porter, M. E. et al. *Upgrading New Zealand's Competitive Advantage (The 'Porter Project')*. Auckland: Oxford.

Department of Employment, Education and Training 1991 *Australia's Language: The Australian Language and Literacy Policy. Vols 1 and 2*. Canberra: Australian Government Publishing Service.

Education for the 21st Century: A discussion document. 1993 Wellington: Ministry of Education.

Education for the 21st Century. 1994 Wellington: Ministry of Education.

Education Statistics of New Zealand 1992 (Annual). Wellington: Ministry of Education (contains data for 1991).

Goff, Hon. P. 1990 Speech to 'Living languages in Aotearoa'. Speech notes for an address given at the Wellington College of Education, Tuesday, 28 August.

Languages for All. Submission on a National Languages Policy for New Zealand. Auckland New Zealand Association of Language Teachers 1991. Reprinted in full in *New Zealand Language Teacher 17.2/3* (1991). 23–35.

Lo Bianco, J. 1987 *National Policy on Languages*. Canberra: Australian Government Publishing Service.

McPherson, J. and Corson, D. 1989 *Language Policy across the Curriculum: Eight Case Studies of School-based Policy Development*. Palmerston North: Massey University.

The Maori Language Act 1987. Wellington: Government Printer.

The National Curriculum of New Zealand: A Discussion Document 1991. Wellington: Ministry of Education.

The New Zealand Curriculum Framework 1993. Wellington: Ministry of Education.

New Zealand *Herald*. 28 December 1991. Auckland: Wilson and Horton.

NZLP Report: Analysis of Responses 1992. Unpublished document. Wellington: Ministry of Education. (Released under the *Official Information Act*.)

Peddie, R. A. 1991a 'Coming—Ready or not?' Language policy development in New Zealand. In *Language Problems and Language Planning 15.1*. 25–42.

Peddie, R. A. 1991b Comparative studies in education: lessons for New Zealand? In *Education Models from Overseas*. Wellington: New Zealand Planning Council.

Peddie, R. A. 1991c Language, culture and curriculum: New Zealand in comparative perspective. In J. R. Liesch (ed.) *Culture, Education and the State*. Sydney: Proceedings of the 19th Annual Conference of the Australian and New Zealand Comparative and International Education Society (ANZCIES).

Peddie, R. A. 1991d *One, Two, or Many? The Development and Implementation of Languages Policy in New Zealand*. Report to the Ministry of Education. Auckland: University of Auckland Education Department. vi + 85.

Peddie, R. A. 1992a How Far Have We Come? How Far to Go? Languages Policy Development in New Zealand. Paper delivered at the 3rd National Conference on Community Languages and English for Speakers of Other Languages, 31 August to 3 September, Auckland.

Peddie, R. A. 1992b Language and languages policy in New Zealand: defining the issues. In *English in Aotearoa 18*. 40–50.

Peddie, R. A. 1993 *From Policy to Practice: The Implementation of Languages Policies in Victoria, Australia, and New Zealand*. Report to the New Zealand Ministry of Education. Auckland: University of Auckland. viii + 137.

Peddie, R. A. and Penfold, V. B. 1987 *Chance for Tomorrow: An Evaluation of the English Language Teaching Unit, Mount Roskill Grammar School, Auckland*. Auckland: Report to the New Zealand Department of Education, Wellington.

Towards a National Languages Policy for New Zealand. *Hei putake mo tetahi kaupapa reo mo Aotearoa*. 1989. Unpublished paper. Wellington: National Languages Policy Secretariat, September.

Waite, J. 1992 Aoteareo: *Speaking for Ourselves*. Parts 1 and 2. Wellington: Ministry of Education.

PART III

TEACHING WITHIN LANGUAGE AND LANGUAGE-IN-EDUCATION POLICIES

CHAPTER 8

SOCIAL JUSTICE IN THE WORK OF ESL TEACHERS

David Corson[17]
Modern Language Centre, Ontario Institute for Studies in Education,
Toronto, Canada

I have a certain ambivalence in approaching the topic of English as a second language and its role in national language policies. This is because, on the one hand, I am very aware of the great need for quality ESL programs in the countries that we are discussing in this volume and I am familiar with the distinguished record that ESL professionals have in providing those programs. On the other hand, I am also aware of a negative function that ESL can have in unwittingly serving the interests of ideological movements, such as the English-Only movement in the United States (Crawford 1992), through blocking the development of just and fair bilingual programs that maintain the first language of minority first language speakers—and doing so for the children's own good.

As a result, in the first part of this chapter on sociopolitical concerns, I want to encourage Teachers of English to Speakers of Other Languages (TESOL) affiliates to enlarge their domain of concern by considering wider social justice issues that relate very much to the use of English in schools. In Canada, I am heavily involved providing workshops for Boards of Education on "anti-bias practices for ESL teachers". There is growing interest here in anti-racism and all aspects of anti-bias policies and practices. So I am trying to promote reform and change in ESL practices, and thus indirectly in national policies. As we now know, the best way to change the structures that affect action in human affairs is to change the discourse about those structures.

[17] I thank Barbara Burnaby, Jean Handscombe, and Merrill Swain for their helpful comments on an initial draft of this paper.

The key point in what follows is this: education often routinely represses, dominates, and disempowers language users whose practices differ
from the norms it establishes. Clearly, the forms of language that schools
value are not available to many children who come from class, gender,
or cultural backgrounds that differ from dominant norms. Yet, most of
the time, schools still operate as if all children had ready access to the
dominant norm or should be expected to gain access to it. This unjust
misdirection in policy routinely disadvantages those girls and minority
students who value and use discourse norms or language codes that
attract a lowly status in conventional schooling. In this chapter I have
tried to provide an outline of these ideas under four central themes: (1)
minority cultural groups and language policy, (2) bilingual education
and social justice, (3) minority social groups and non-standard discourse, and (4) gender and the discourse norms of women and girls.

Theme 1: Minority cultural groups and language policy

Many educational difficulties confronting children from minority cultures are related to sociolinguistic interference (Gumperz 1977). But
teachers often are unaware of the impact on school learning of subtle
differences in the language norms minority children bring to school.
Teachers sometimes regard minority children as unresponsive or dis-
ruptive, as slow learners, or as candidates for ESL programs; they overlook the reality that members of a minority culture bring an understanding of their culture's own participant norms for interaction that
may be very different from the dominant pattern (Cazden 1988, 1989;
Corson 1993). These norms are expressions of the minority culture's values; they provide informal rules that govern speaking, listening, and
turn-taking behaviours. Many studies now confirm the prevalence of
inappropriate classroom and school contexts of interaction for minority
children (eg, Cazden 1988; Luke et al. 1994; Malcolm 1982; Michaels
1981; Philips 1983; Scollon and Scollon 1981; Smitherman 1977).
Information about these subtle differences in minority children's language norms rarely appears in the professional training curriculum of
teachers. This information often falls outside the taken-for-granted reality of professional policy and practice in education, even for teachers
such as ESL professionals who are centrally concerned with issues of
language.

So my questions arising from theme 1 are: Should ESL teachers know more about the impact of cultural and language norms? How can they get access to useful and up-to-date information on the discourse norms of culturally different students in their classes? How can they adjust their practices and policies if they feel they need to?

Theme 2: Bilingual education and social justice

The conventional policy in education for dealing with speakers of minority languages has been to ignore the first language of minority children and to replace it with the dominant language of education (Romaine 1989; Skutnabb-Kangas 1981), which in the TESOL context is of course English. Yet, an educational system serving a multilingual society but providing only monolingual schooling clearly infringes on the language rights of minority language speakers (Corson 1993). Furthermore, evidence now supports the view that second language students can gain important educational benefits when their first language is maintained. Bilingual schooling itself has cognitive advantages for the learner (eg, Baker 1988; Crystal 1987). The maintenance of minority children's first languages is an effective aid in promoting their learning of the majority language, in developing their self-confidence, and in improving access to further education (eg, Appel and Muysken 1987; Campos and Keatinge 1988; Chamot 1988; Corson 1990; Cummins 1994; Fitzpatrick 1987; Hagman and Lahdenperä 1988; Vallen and Stijnen 1987).

So my questions arising from theme 2 are: How can ESL teachers make contact with recent research developments in this dynamic area of bilingual education? What changes in policies and practices at the TESOL association level might follow from recent research? Should ESL teachers adjust their professional practices to become bilingual educationists rather than just second language teachers?

Theme 3: Minority social groups and non-standard discourse

Injustice occurs when those who do not use the standard version of a language enter an educational system in which the standard version is considered "correct" (Bourdieu 1991; Dannequin 1987; Labov 1982). Some children starting out in school have more of this resource than do others and are consistently rewarded for its possession. Standard English is often uncritically used as the model of excellence against which other varieties of English are measured, and non-standard users come to see their own varieties as of lesser worth. In most school settings, the standard variety is more practical, not because of its "correctness" but because of its greater "appropriateness" (Winch 1989). But in some contexts there are also strong justice grounds for preferring a non-standard variety over the standard as the language of schooling (Milroy and Milroy 1978); and in every context it is important to value the language variety that children bring from their home community into the schools, and to do so in ways that enhance all children's critical awareness concerning language varieties (Corson 1993).

An additional issue is the effect of non-standard varieties in creating teacher stereotypes (Hewstone and Giles 1986). The evidence of language itself is central in activating negative teacher attitudes towards the speech of culturally and socially different children, thus affecting teacher expectations, which in turn affect pupil performance (J. Edwards 1989). In fact, teachers' perceptions of children's non-standard speech produces negative expectations about the children's personalities, social backgrounds, and academic abilities (V. Edwards 1986; Fasold 1984; Giles 1987).

So my questions arising from theme 3 are: Where do ESL professionals stand on the issue of correctness versus appropriateness in English usage? How can ESL programs address the genuine ESL needs of students who speak a variety of English that is markedly different from the variety given high status in their school? How can all students become critically aware of the sociocultural and historical factors that give high status to one form of English and not to other varieties?

Theme 4: Gender and the discourse norms of women and girls

Cross-cultural studies of gender and language as well as studies of language socialisation confirm that language plays a highly diverse role in the social construction of gender and that the effects of socialisation through language appear very early in children's lives (Gleason 1987; Philips et al. 1987; Corson 1993). Many key areas of gender injustice in schools relate to language: gender differences in teacher–pupil and pupil–pupil interactions; the use of sexist language, textbooks and reading schemes; and the choice of discourse norms for use in classroom interaction and for wider assessment (Blackmore and Kenway 1994; Cheshire and Jenkins 1991; Kelly 1988; Klann-Delius 1987; Thorne 1986). Differences in the discourse norms of men and women can be traced back to differences between boys and girls that are largely modelled on differences between men and women (Maltz and Borker 1983). These differences are reinforced by current school language policies. Moreover, many girls may be excluded from participation in intellectually developing activities at higher levels of education because those activities favour discourse norms closer to those of many men and boys. In addition, studies that address the interaction of gender, culture, and language highlight the special injustices that girls from minority backgrounds often encounter (Biggs and Edwards 1991; Corson 1993; Jones 1987; Michaels 1981).

So my questions arising from theme 4 are: How can ESL professionals grapple in their practices with these issues, which impact most heavily on girls from cultural minorities? Is there a leadership role in this, and all the other theme areas, that ESL teachers can take in schools? Can equitable "language policies across the curriculum" be developed that have a direct impact on school and classroom practices for all students?

TESOL and the immigrant language minorities of five English-speaking countries

Because of the great population shifts that have occurred over the last two or three generations, great attention is now given to national language policies. These shifts highlight language issues that formerly lay submerged in societies, even in those countries where there were always significant language minorities. Reporting from his studies of OECD countries, Stacy Churchill (1986) sees major changes occurring everywhere in national attitudes toward minorities. He sees the recent development of an international climate of opinion favouring the more open and tolerant treatment of minorities as the most potent factor in this move. As an example, he uses his own country, providing a case study that links improvements in the treatment of the Francophone minority in Canada with changes in the structures of social life brought about by increased prosperity and by urbanisation.

In modern societies, there are three main types of minorities: ancestral peoples, "established" minorities, and "new" minorities. The first of these—the ancestral peoples—includes those groups long established in their native countries, peoples such as the Sami, Maori, Inuit, American Indians, and Aborigines. Increasingly, in places where indigenous peoples are to be found, racist attitudes are becoming socially unacceptable, and people of mixed ancestry are identifying more readily with the ancestral minority than once might have been the case. In a place like Tasmania, for example, where the indigenous minority all but disappeared a century ago, a vigorous minority action group has surfaced that takes its lead from larger minority groups elsewhere like the New Zealand Maori, whose presence as a cultural force has never been in doubt.

Other examples of "established" minorities are the Catalans in Spain, the Acadian French in the United States, the Bretons in France, or Canadian Francophones. "New" minorities are more recent arrivals. They include those who are immigrants in the legal sense; refugees, such as the "boat people" fleeing from Indo-Chinese countries, and other statutory refugees; foreign workers living semi-permanently in their new homes; and expatriates serving in countries that are tied in a loose community with one another, such as the British Commonwealth, the Nordic States, or the European Community.

In their *explicit* or *tacit* national language policies, each of the five English-speaking countries addressed in this volume (Australia, Canada, New Zealand, the United Kingdom, and the United States,) approaches the language problems of its new minorities from a "language deficit position" (Churchill 1986). In practice, this means that language policies in the five countries fall under one or more of the following three categories:

1. The national language policy sees the new language minority groups as *lacking English,* and the typical policy response is to provide supplementary teaching in English (ie, ESL) with a rapid transition expected to the use of English

2. The national language policy sees the minority groups' deficit as also linked to family status; so an additional policy response is to provide special measures to help minority students adjust to the majority society—measures such as aids, tutors, psychologists, social workers, career advisers

3. The national language policy sees the minority groups' deficit as linked to disparities in esteem between each group's culture and the majority culture, so additional policy responses are to include multi-cultural teaching programs for all children, to sensitise teachers to minority needs, and to revise textbooks and other learning materials to eliminate racial stereotyping.

With only rare exceptions in limited contexts (eg, in the United States, see Garcia and Otheguy 1987; in New Zealand, see May 1994; in Australia, see Kalantzis et al. 1990; in the United Kingdom, see Fitzpatrick 1987; and in Canada, see Corson and Lemay 1996, Gillett 1987), language policies for immigrant minorities in all five countries are located at one of the three levels mentioned above. But elsewhere, in countries like Belgium, Switzerland, Finland, and Sweden, where more established minorities exist, more just and enlightened language prac-tices prevail. Similarly in most of Canada, fair practices are available for official language minorities (ie, as distinct from immigrant and aborigi-nal minorities) (Corson and Lemay 1996). These more enlightened poli-cies provide three more sophisticated and equitable responses:

4. The national language policy sees the premature loss of the minority tongue as an inhibiting transition to learning the majority tongue, so an additional policy response is to provide some study of minority languages in schools, perhaps as an early or occasional medium of transitional instruction

5. The national language policy sees the minority groups' languages threatened with extinction as community languages if they are not supported, so the policy response is to provide the minority lan-guages as media of instruction, usually exclusively in the early years of schooling

6. The national language policy sees the minority and majority lan-guages as having equal rights in society, with special support avail-able for the less viable languages, so policy responses include recog-nition of a minority language as an official language, separate educa-tional institutions for language groups, opportunities for all children to learn both languages voluntarily, and support beyond educational systems.

Only the very old bilingual or multilingual OECD states have reached level 6 (Churchill 1986). Some ambiguity exists in other countries—notably in Canada, which has no national coordinating body for education, much less for coordinating language policies. As a result, Canadian policies differ markedly across provincial boundaries and school districts. First language support, for the established Francophone minorities outside Québec and for the established Anglophone minorities inside Québec, is generally protected by the *Official Languages Act*. But new minorities, including the 250 000 new immigrants and refugees that enter Canada each year are almost universally asked to transfer to an official language (English or French) as their language of education (Corson and Lemay 1996). Sweden provides the only level 5 enrichment program in the world for its labour immigrant Finnish minority (Skutnabb-Kangas 1981), although in Sweden, educational practice in some places may be lagging behind educational policy. In other aspects, it may still be at level 4.

In New Zealand, the *Maori Language Act* of 1987 declared Maori to be an official language of the country and anyone now has the right to speak Maori in legal proceedings. So New Zealand has begun to move towards the enrichment levels 5 and 6, but only in relation to its ancestral Maori minority. In its language policies for the large Pacific Island minorities and other new settlers, New Zealand is still at level 1 or 2, and even the provision of ESL instruction is at relatively unsophisticated levels.

The United States' *Bilingual Education Act* legislation seems to locate that country firmly at level 4, although the responses of most schools and school districts themselves seem to be at a much lower stage. That Act deals with "limited English proficient" (LEP) students of three types: (1) persons born outside the United States or persons whose native language is not English, (2) persons in whose environment a non-English language is dominant, and (3) Native Americans in whose environment a non-English language has significantly affected their proficiency in English. These three categories are broadly similar to the three types of linguistic minorities mentioned previously. In dealing with these three types of LEP students, all of the school districts surveyed by Chamot (1988) have tried to develop students' English proficiency so that the students can participate successfully in all-English instruction. Nearly all districts report that their goal is the development of the academic skills needed for school achievement, while only a small minority of schools indicate that the development or maintenance of the students' first language is a goal. One major reason for these policies has been the belief that they would provide bilingual children with equal access to the educational system and give them achievement scores equal to monolingual children. Achievement score disparities have not been removed, however (Philips 1983).

In practice then, the United States is located at levels 1 or 2. There may be major obstacles to producing much advance on this, given the fact that English has been repeatedly fostered in that country to create an "American ethnicity" (Fishman 1967), even though there have always been high concentrations of people using languages other than English to conduct their affairs: Spanish in the Southwest, in Puerto Rico, and in New York; French in some parts of Louisiana and Maine; and German in Pennsylvania and Ohio. Although USA census figures reveal more than 65 languages spoken in that country, in addition to the many indigenous tongues, and although a presidential commission has created a National Council on Foreign Language Teaching and International Studies, the image of a rigorous monolingualism is still promoted in the United States. However, much the same was said of Australia before the 1970s, and the changes that have occurred there in the past generation offer some hope of development in rigorously monocultural societies elsewhere.

Its major Celtic areas apart, Britain has much in common in its development with the United States. Britain is at level 3 in the attitudes to multiculturalism that curriculum specialists advocate, but it is only at level 1 in its treatment of new settler minority language users. Tosi (1988) finds it paradoxical that bilingualism is discussed in schools and colleges as a subject of multicultural interest, yet it is still regarded as educationally undesirable. Britain's Swann Report (1985) rejects bilingual education or mother tongue maintenance at an official school level. Instead, schools are urged (where possible) to teach community languages as subjects equal in status to foreign languages in the wider curriculum and to allow communities to use schools as a resource for the transmission of community languages. At least 28 different languages are being taught in over 500 community language schools. Local education authorities differ in their policies, some stressing transition and others allowing for some pluralism. Reid (1988) reports that local authorities have begun the practice of "mainstreaming" students, using ESL teachers in supportive roles focusing on the standard curriculum.

New settler community languages in Britain receive some recognition, but only in the early stages of schooling to ease transition to English. True bilingual education has no status, nor is there official recognition of the cultural resource represented by the presence of large numbers of speakers of non-indigenous languages. Indigenous minorities are much better provided for in Britain than non-indigenous groups, but these provisions have been won only after a long struggle by the speakers themselves.

Australia is located at several levels at once. For example, on the evidence of the treatment of many users of Aboriginal languages and some community language users, Australia is at levels 4 or 5. Its policies of multiculturalism as a response to the needs of other minority groups locate it at level 3. Although it does not need to address two official languages in its policies, as does Canada, Australia has a complex language situation: it is a country where more than 100 community languages are in regular use, where 50 Aboriginal languages still survive, and where for a large minority of the population English is not the mother tongue. In the face of this social and cultural complexity, Australia in the 1970s and 1980s changed its course away from the shortsighted monocultural values about language issues that had previously directed policies at the national level. Having experimented extensively with national policies based on the vague ideology of multiculturalism, and following the advice and pressure of its growing multicultural communities, Australia is increasingly seeing its language pluralism as a valuable national resource that enriches cultural and intellectual life and that is also invaluable in its potential as a resource in international trade (Lo Bianco 1987). As part of this change, there are strong signs that an ethnic revival has occurred in the country. People seem more ready to take pride in their language proficiency and their ethnic background (Clyne 1988). A more diverse and healthily volatile language situation appears to be developing, with a number of new and expanding speech communities.

ESL in pluralist settings: social justice and the school

If my treatment of ESL seems a little out of balance, this short discussion may redress things. The centrepiece of a national language policy remains the degree of importance the nation gives to the country's dominant language(s). Other issues related to other languages may be more important for those who have an interest in those languages, but in mainly monolingual societies the problems that people have with the majority language will inevitably be the dominant ones for a policy to consider. In all countries, a large minority of majority language users may need help in the skills of using that language in certain contexts, functions, styles, or modes of language-in-use. Adult literacy programs are an enduring need in even the most educationally well served of countries. Mother tongue teaching in schools is the major part of the ambit of influence that a national language policy covers. A second language may be a desirable acquisition for everyone, but a firm grasp of the first language, in all its functions and styles, is essential. Mastery of the mother tongue has priority if people are to have a voice in society and control over their own affairs.

Yet, with a well-designed and explicit national policy, less scope exists for a conflict of interest between the needs of mother tongue speakers and second language needs. Enhancing the teaching of second languages while still strengthening the mother tongue across the country is possible. The reasons for this are only now beginning to emerge in studies of bilingualism and second language learning: the learner who is reasonably proficient in a first language has that proficiency increased, not diminished, by studying a second language.

Clearly, most decisions about minority languages and ESL in the pluralist societies this volume covers will need to be made and implemented *at the level of the school*. Devolving decision-making in this way, in any act of social policy, seems consistent with modern accounts of social justice and policy (Corson 1993). When talking about justice and fairness, we need as many conceptions of justice as there are distinct possible conditions of society or subsets of society or culture. This conclusion is consistent, too, with the snowballing trend towards parent and community involvement in school decision-making: local minority communities must be involved in deciding the shape and direction of their children's schools if the cultural pluralism that exists almost everywhere in these five countries is to be recognised and provided for in just policies.

In consort with national policies and projects about language and languages, I suggest that a movement to create a climate for the development of *language policies across the curriculum* of individual schools is a reasonable and proper course for education in pluralist societies to be setting (Corson 1990). The development of a school language policy depends on a number of factors—within the school's ambit of control: a developing awareness among teaching staff to the role of language in learning across the curriculum, a willingness to undertake some research into the language needs of a particular school community, a familiarity with the theory (ie, knowledge) that relates to language problems, the openness to consult with parents and the wider society, and the leadership of the school executive and the enthusiasm of the whole school community in making the policy development process work. Obviously, establishing the place of ESL in the classroom, in the school, and in the community is central to this kind of local policy-making.

References

Appel, R. and Muysken, P. 1987 *Language Contact and Bilingualism*. London: Edward Arnold.

Assembly of First Nations 1988 *Tradition and Education: Towards a Vision of Our Future*. Ottawa.

Baker, C. 1988 *Key Issues in Bilingualism and Bilingual Education*. Clevedon, Avon, and Philadelphia: Multilingual Matters.

Barman, J., Hebert, Y. and McCaskill, D. (eds) 1986 *Indian Education in Canada. Vol. 1 The Legacy*. Vancouver: University of British Columbia Press.

Biggs, N. and Edwards, V. 1991 'I treat them all the same': teacher–pupil talk in multiethnic classrooms. *Language and Education 5.1.* 61–176.

Blackmore, J. and Kenway, J. 1994 Changing schools, teachers and curriculum: but what about the girls? In D. Corson (ed.) *Discourse and Power in Educational Organizations*. Cresskill, NJ: Hampton Press.

Bourdieu, P. 1991 *Language and Symbolic Power*. Cambridge: Basil Blackwell.

Campos, S. and Keatinge, H. 1988 The Carpinteria language minority student experience: from theory, to practice, to success. In T. Skutnabb-Kangas and J. Cummins (eds) *Minority Education: From Shame to Struggle*. Clevedon, Avon: Multilingual Matters.

Cazden, C. 1988 *Classroom Discourse: The Language of Teaching and Learning*. Portsmouth, NH: Heinemann.

Cazden, C. 1989 Richmond Road: a multilingual/multicultural primary school in Auckland, New Zealand. *Language and Education 3.* 143–66.

Chamot, A. 1988 Bilingualism in education and bilingual education: the state of the art in the United States. *Journal of Multilingual and Multicultural Development 9.* 11–35.

Cheshire, J. and Jenkins, N. 1991 Gender issues in the GCSE Oral English Examination: Part 2. *Language and Education 5.* 19–40.

Churchill, S. 1986 *The Education of Linguistic and Cultural Minorities in OECD Countries*. Philadelphia: Multilingual Matters.

Clyne, M. 1988 Community language in the home: a first report. *Vox 1*. 22–27.

Connors, B. 1984 A multicultural curriculum as action for social justice. In S. Shapson and V. D'Oyley (eds) *Bilingual and Multicultural Education: Canadian Perspectives*. Clevedon, Avon: Multilingual Matters.

Corson, D. 1990 *Language Policy across the Curriculum*. Clevedon, Avon: Multilingual Matters.

Corson, D. 1993 *Language, Minority Education and Gender: Linking Social Justice and Power*. Toronto: OISE Press; Clevedon, Avon: Multilingual Matters.

Corson, D. 1995 *Using English Words*. Amsterdam: Kluwer Academic.

Corson, D. 1995 *Discourse and Power in Educational Organizations*. Cresskill, NJ: Hampton Press.

Corson, D. and Lemay, S. 1996 *Social Justice and Language Policy in Education: The Canadian Research*. Toronto: OISE Press.

Crawford, J. 1992 *Hold Your Tongue: Bilingualism and the Politics of 'English Only'*. Reading, MA: Addison-Wesley.

Crystal, D. 1987 *The Cambridge Encyclopedia of Language*. Cambridge: Cambridge University Press.

Cummins, J. 1994 Discursive power in educational policy and practice for culturally diverse students. In D. Corson (ed.) *Discourse and Power in Educational Organizations*. Cresskill, NJ: Hampton Press.

Cummins, J. and Swain, M. 1986 *Bilingualism in Education: Aspects of Theory Research and Practice*. London: Longman.

Dannequin, C. 1987 *Les enfants baillonnés*: the teaching of French as mother tongue in elementary school. Language and Education 1. 15–31.

Edwards, J. 1989 *Language and Disadvantage: Studies in Disorders of Communication*. 2nd ed. London: Cole and Whurr.

Edwards, V. 1986 *Language in a Black Community*. Clevedon, Avon: Multilingual Matters.

Fasold, R. 1984 *The Sociolinguistics of Society*. Oxford: Basil Blackwell.

Fishman, J. 1967 Bilingualism with and without diglossia: diglossia with and without bilingualism. *Journal of Social Issues 23*. 29–38.

Fitzpatrick, F. 1987 *The Open Door*. Clevedon, Avon: Multilingual Matters.

Garcia, O. and Otheguy, R. 1987 The bilingual education of Cuban-American children in Dade County's ethnic schools. *Language and Education 1*. 83–95.

Giles, H., Taylor, D. and Bourhis, R. 1988 Research on language attitudes. In U. Ammon, N. Dittmar and K. Mattheier (eds) *Sociolinguistics*. Berlin: de Gruyter.

Gillett, J. S. 1987 Ethnic bilingual education for Canada's minority groups. *Canadian Modern Language Review 43*. 337–55.

Gleason, J. B. 1987 Sex differences in parent–child interaction. In S. Philips, S. Steele, and C. Tanz (eds) *Language, Gender, and Sex in Comparative Perspective*. Cambridge: Cambridge University Press.

Griffith, A. and Smith, D. 1987 Constructing cultural knowledge. In J. Gaskell and A. McLaren (eds) *Women and Education: A Canadian Perspective.* Calgary: Detselig.

Gumperz, J. 1977 Sociocultural knowledge in conversational inference. In M. Saville-Troike (ed.) *Twenty-Eighth Annual Roundtable Monograph Series in Language and Linguistics.* Washington, DC: Georgetown University Press.

Hagman, T. and Lahdenperä, J. 1988 Nine years of Finnish-medium education in Sweden: what happens afterwards? The education of minority children in Botkyrka. In T. Skutnabb-Kangas and J. Cummins (eds) *Minority Education: From Shame to Struggle.* Clevedon, Avon: Multilingual Matters.

Hewstone, M. and Giles, H. 1986 Social groups and social stereotypes in intergroup communication. In W. Gudykunst (ed.) *Intergroup Communication.* London: Edward Arnold.

Holm, A. and Holm, W. 1990 Rock Point, a Navajo way to go to school: a valediction. In C. Cazden and C. Snow (eds) *English Plus: Issues in Bilingual Education.* Newbury Park, CA: Sage Publications.

Jones, A. 1987 Which girls are 'learning to lose'? In S. Middleton (ed.) *Women and Education in Aotearoa.* Wellington: Allen and Unwin.

Kalantzis, M., Cope, B., Noble, G. and Poynting, S. 1990 *Cultures of Schooling: Pedagogies for Cultural Difference and Social Access.* London: Falmer.

Kelly, A. 1988 Gender differences in teacher–pupil interactions: a meta-analytic review. *Research in Education 39.* 1–23.

Klann-Delius, G. 1987 Sex and language. In U. Ammon, N. Dittmar and K. Mattheier (eds) *Sociolinguistics.* Berlin: de Gruyter.

Labov, W. 1982 Objectivity and commitment in linguistic science: the case of the Black English trial in Ann Arbor. *Language in Society 11.* 165–201.

Leavitt, R. 1991 Language and cultural content in native education. *Canadian Modem Language Review 47.* 266–79.

Lewis, M. and Simon, R. 1987 A discourse not intended for her. In J. Gaskell and A. McLaren (eds) *Women and Education: A Canadian Perspective.* Calgary: Detselig.

Lo Bianco, J. 1987 *National Policy on Languages.* Canberra: Australian Government Publishing Service.

Luke, A., Kale, J. and Garbutcheon Singh, M. 1994 Talking difference: discourses on Aboriginal identity in grade one classrooms. In D. Corson (ed.) *Discourse and Power in Educational Organizations.* Cresskill, NJ: Hampton Press.

Malcolm, I. 1982 Speech events of the Aboriginal classroom. *International Journal of the Sociology of Language. 36.* 115–34.

Maltz, D. and Borker, R. 1983 A cultural approach to male–female miscommunication. In J. Gumperz (ed.) *Language and Social Identity.* Cambridge: Cambridge University Press. 195–216.

May, S. 1994 *Making Multicultural Education Work*. Clevedon, Avon: Multilingual Matters.

Michaels, S. 1981 'Sharing time': children's narrative styles and differential access to literacy. *Language in Society 10*. 4–42.

Milroy, J. and Milroy, L. 1978 Belfast: change and variation in an urban vernacular. In P. Trudgill (ed.) *Sociolinguistic Patterns in British English*. London: Arnold.

Philips, S. 1983 *The Invisible Culture: Communication in Classroom and Community on the Warm Springs Indian Reservation*. New York: Longman.

Philips, S., Steele, S. and Tanz, C. (eds) 1987 *Language, Gender, and Sex in Comparative Perspective*. Cambridge: Cambridge University Press.

Reid, E. 1988 Linguistic minorities and language education: the English experience. *Journal of Multilingual and Multicultural Development 9*. 181–91, 220–23.

Romaine, S. 1989 *Bilingualism*. Oxford: Basil Blackwell.

Scollon, R. and Scollon, S. 1981 *Narrative Literacy and Face in Inter-Ethnic Communication*. Norwood, NJ: Ablex.

Skutnabb-Kangas, T. 1981 *Bilingualism or Not: The Education of Minorities*. Clevedon, Avon: Multilingual Matters.

Skutnabb-Kangas, T. and Cummins, J. (eds) 1988 *Minority Education: From Shame to Struggle*. Clevedon, Avon: Multilingual Matters.

Smith, D. 1987 An analysis of ideological structures and how women are excluded. In J. Gaskell and A. McLaren *(eds) Women and Education: A Canadian Perspective*. Calgary: Detselig.

Smitherman, G. 1977 *Talkin' and Testifyin': The Language of Black America*. Boston: Houghton Mifflin.

Thorne, B. 1986 Girls and boys together. . .but mostly apart: gender arrangements in elementary schools. In W. Hartup and Z. Rubin (eds) *Relationships and Development*. Hillsdale, NJ: Lawrence Erlbaum.

Tosi, A. 1988 The new approach to bilingualism in multicultural education in England. In T. Skutnabb-Kangas and J. Cummins (eds) *Minority Education: From Shame to Struggle*. Clevedon, Avon: Multilingual Matters.

Vallen, T. and Stijnen, S. 1987 Language and educational success of indigenous and non-indigenous minority students in the Netherlands. *Language and Education 1*. 109–24.

Winch, C. 1989 Standard English, normativity and the Cox Committee Report. *Language and Education 3*. 275–93.

CHAPTER 9

THE ROLES AND RESPONSIBILITIES OF ESL TEACHERS WITHIN NATIONAL LANGUAGE POLICIES

William Eggington
Brigham Young University, USA

As this book approaches its final editing and printing stage, some English-dominant nations have implemented policies, or have engaged in serious debate aimed, at "protecting" the English language as the formal or informal national language in the hope of fostering national unity or achieving national sociopolitical goals. The United States Congress is currently debating at least three bills aimed at declaring English the official language. US Senator Dole has made the aims of "US English" movement a presidential campaign issue, and a recent *US News and World Report* (September 25 1995) addressed the questions "One Nation, One Language?" and "Would making English the nation's official language unite the country or divide it?" as its cover issue (38–48). New Zealand has implemented a policy where non-English speaking immigrants are required to deposit a $20 000 bond which they will forfeit if they do not pass a government imposed English examination within a year (*EL Gazette*, September 1995:1). In Australia, the debate continues over the ongoing thrust of current language policy which has redefined national language policy. The policy once promoted English and other community languages as part of a community model. A redefined policy now focuses on English literacy and language and the development of key foreign languages within economic rationalistic models.

For me, New Zealand's example succinctly personalizes the issue under discussion in these closing remarks; namely, the roles and responsibilities of ESL teachers within the national language policies discussed in this volume. In the late 1980s, I was asked to be part of a team charged to develop a prototype listening examination for a new International English Language Testing System (IELTS). I gladly accepted the responsibility (and the money), and contributed to the development of the prototype. Now, seven years later, I find that the IELTS Listening Test is the New Zealand government's examining instrument that will either allow some struggling immigrant to regain $20 000, or cause that immigrant to lose $20 000. I have sat for many examinations in my lifetime, but never one that would cost me $20 000 if I were to fail. I should imagine that, for most, the test anxiety would be overwhelming. It probably would be for me. Had I known that the test I helped develop would be used as part of such a damaging and unproductive language policy, would I have offered my services? The answer to this question demands a more general process of enquiry which could result in a set of questions including:

- What responsibilities do ESL teachers have in implementing a language policy that may be oppressive, foolish or, in their view, just plain wrong?
- What responsibilities do ESL teachers have in the development, evaluation and/or alteration of a language policy?
- What responsibilities do ESL teachers have in informing their students of the policies which directly impact them?

Although a full response to these questions lies beyond the scope of this present volume, some insights into the divergent views can be derived from the articles herein. Kaplan, in his foreword, states that "only after professionalism has been achieved within the profession can there be any hope of influencing national language policies". On the other hand, Wren suggests that ESL teachers, through their professional organizations, can influence policy, a view tentatively verified by Bourne's review of the influence of teachers in the formation of British language policy. In regards to the United States, McGroarty argues for language teachers seeking "to influence politicians through provision of timely, specific and informed critiques of possible alternatives" within informed advocacy principles, but cautions that ESL teachers are only one voice among many vested groups and individuals. Other contributors to this volume have either addressed the issue tangentially, or have agreed with a "one voice among many" position.

Given the complexity of community and professional attitudes held toward language, such variation is not surprising. As may be gleaned by my contribution to this volume, a historical analysis of English language metaphors, I have lately been interested in the sociopolitical history of the English language. I get excited when I rediscover and re-teach that, for example, the Australian morphological variant, *me and me sister*, or the US Southern variant *I'm a-fixin' to go* have over a 500 year dialectal history. For much of this time, these forms have been stigmatized, their speakers stereotyped as lazy, lower class, poor learners, etc. And yet in the face of all this pressure, and in the face of a host of covert and overt mini-language policies implemented to eradicate such "oddities", these forms survive among a significant group of people. For some reason, these people needed these linguistic forms as part of their sociocultural identity, and so they remain, often as part of speakers' register repertoire.

Many of these people are part of a larger group labelled by Lave (1988) as JPFs (just plain folks). Lave's ethnographic studies of the differences in problem solving strategies between school contexts and JPFs in everyday activities reveals a tendency for JPFs to solve real world problems through very pragmatic, contextualised procedures. In other words, when JPFs are given sufficient information to make informed decisions, and freedom to exercise intuitive problem solving techniques, they often accomplish tasks far more efficiently than others using school-based solutions driven by decontextualised procedural models. Often, JPFs stubbornly refuse to change their behaviour in accordance with theory and/or research driven alternative solutions or ways.

Given this observation, language planners need to be aware that if they wish to alter the existing, socially constructed linguistic make-up of a community, they are tampering with a status quo that has often been developed by JPFs to benefit a significant proportion of JPFs. Unless large numbers of JPFs are "converted" to the alternative new solution, social resistance can eventually pull any language policy back to the general community's status quo, its comfortable linguistic centre of gravity. Of course, I am guilty of over simplification, but still this process may explain some of the feeling behind the current scaling back of bilingual education programs and the community based multilingual movement in the United States and in Australia. Consequently, for a language policy to be successful in the long term, it must create a way for JPFs to "own" the policy to the point where the alternative new policy becomes the obvious pragmatic, long term, "COMMON sense" solution.

One method of achieving this objective is for the language policy to be "sold" to the community. Sold by whom? Perhaps sold by the front-line deliverers of that policy directly to those most affected by the policy. And, in most language policies, language teachers and other language educators are the front-line deliverers of the policy. Here then is a role for ESL and other language teachers. Of course, no one can sell anything as personal as a language policy successfully without agreeing with that policy. For professionals such as language teachers, the best way to ensure that teachers will agree with a policy is to bring them into the language planning process from its beginning stages. This means that language teachers need to become experts in much more than classroom bound teaching strategies. They need to understand public policy procedures, sociolinguistic research and the existing policies under which they and their students are currently functioning. Hopefully, this book has helped address aspects of the latter issue.

Reference

Lave, J. 1988 *Cognition in Practice*. Boston, MA: Cambridge.

Notes on contributors

Jill Bourne is Senior Lecturer in Education at the Open University, UK. Her research interests are language in education, language policy, and educational provision for bilingual pupils. She is currently leading the design and presentation of the first primary postgraduate course in initial teacher training by open and distance learning to be presented in the UK.

David Corson is Professor in the Department of Theory and Policy Studies, and in the Modern Language Centre at the Ontario Institute for Studies in Education. He has taught in universities in Canada, England, Australia and New Zealand, including two years as Commonwealth Relations Trust Visiting Fellow in Curriculum Studies at the University of London Institute of Education. He is Founding Editor of *Language and Education* and General Editor of *The Encyclopedia of Language and Education*.

Alister Cumming is Head of the Modern Language Centre and Associate Professor of Curriculum at the Ontario Institute for Studies in Education at the University of Toronto, Canada. He is currently editor of the journal *Language Learning*. His research and graduate courses focus on curriculum, evaluation, literacy, instruction and learning in second language education.

William Eggington is Associate Professor of English language at Brigham Young University, Utah, USA. Originally from Australia, his research and publication interests involve language policy and planning, cross-cultural literacies and sociocultural aspects of English language teaching.

Robert B. Kaplan is Emeritus Professor of Applied Linguistics and past Director of the American Language Institute at the University of Southern California, USA. He founded the *Annual Review of Applied Linguistics*, and is on the editorial board of the Oxford *International Encyclopedia of Linguistics*. He has served as President of TESOL, ATESL, AAAL, CATESOL and NAFSA. He has published widely in contrastive rhetoric and language policy and planning.

Joseph Lo Bianco, Chief Executive of Language Australia Limited, is the author of Australia's *National Policy on Languages*. He is a member of several national and state language policy bodies, and chairs the Education Group of the Australian National Commission for UNESCO. He has published widely in the areas of language planning, the social and intellectual effects of bilingualism and bilingual education, language politics and multilingualism and public policy.

Mary McGroarty is associate professor of applied linguistics in the English Department at Northern Arizona University, specializing in issues related to the interface of language policy, pedagogy, and assessment. She is the 1996–97 VicePresident of the American Association for Applied Linguistics (AAAL) and is also active in TESOL International.

Roger Peddie is an Associate Professor and Director of the Centre for Continuing Education at the University of Auckland, New Zealand. He has been involved in on-going comparative research on languages policy development and implementation in New Zealand and Victoria, Australia, since 1987. He has also researched and published in the fields of assessment and curriculum.

Helen Wren has been a teacher and program administrator in secondary schools mainstream and intensive English programs and teacher development for the Department of School Education, New South Wales, Australia, since 1975. She was president of her state, and later, national TESOL associations and 1991–92 chair of the Sociopolitical Concerns Standing Committee in the international TESOL association.